PRAISE FOR *DANCING WITH ROBOTS*

Leaders walk the line of dealing with the unknown, building confidence to act in those around them, and operating from principles instead of scripts. Bishop is such a leader. In *Dancing with Robots*, readers will go to the precipice of the immediate future in four intersecting domains: humanity, technology, thinking, and business; 29 strategies take the edge off how to embrace artificial intelligence and technology — yes, to dance with it! Readers from the humanities, business, entrepreneurs, health care, and futurists will appreciate the nuanced stories and sharp focus that support each strategy. In the end, the whole is greater than the sum of each part. Highly recommend.

— MICHAEL R. BLEICH, senior professor and director, Virginia Commonwealth University, Langston Center for Innovation in Quality and Safety

I firmly believe Bill Bishop belongs in the same conversations as those involving Seth Godin, Gary V., and others like them (he's a lot more accessible, too). He has the unique ability to take several marketing and sales ideas/ techniques and marry them with technology, and after 20 minutes be able to distill everything in an easy-to-understand plan. I've never worked with anyone like Bill and recommend anything he writes and ultimately teaches.

— DAVID MARINAC, president and CEO, ABC Packaging Direct and The Oversea Network

I've devoured just about everything Bill Bishop has written. He has the unique ability of distilling complex ideas into simple, doable, and commercial outcomes. Three such ideas I took, and actioned, from his last book were simply to identify a big goal, a big problem, and a signature program to satiate them.

— PÁDRAIC Ó MÁILLE, founder, Smácht Training

D0992688

Dancing with Robots is a timely contribution to our knowledge of how to succeed in the New Economy. His 29 practical strategies, personal insights, and big ideas are a game-changer for business leaders.

— NANCY MACKAY, founder and board member, MacKay CEO Forums

Bill Bishop is the "forward-est" of forward thinkers. If you want to see into the future of AI and automation and gain insights into how you might adapt your business and yourself to what's coming next, you have found the right book. Bill paints a picture of the future that is understandable yet comprehensive enough to help you with strategies to survive and thrive among the coming changes. *Dancing With Robots* is a must-read for entrepreneurs and everyone looking into the future.

— STURDY MCKEE, business coach, SturdyCoaching.com

Bill Bishop helped Turkstra Lumber develop our BIG Idea, the Build-It-Better program. This program has been a big hit with our DIY customers and has moved us away from Old Factory Thinking and into the New Economy. Bishop's *The New Economy Thinker* was a must-read for our entire Team. *Dancing with Robots* is a fascinating book that builds on Bill's concepts outlined in *The New Economy Thinker*. The topic is timely and thought provoking as we move into an uncharted but exciting time to be business leaders. We're all looking forward to moving out of the "factories" and joining the "network."

— JON WAGNER, president, Turkstra Lumber

Bill Bishop has done it again, taking readers on a journey to the future that is entertaining and insightful. *Dancing with Robots* is for anyone seeking to understand the New Economy and helps to explain why our future will be more human — not less. As an educator this book offers hope that the future will be defined not by traditional academic silos but by big ideas that require co-creation, our human curiosity and creativity, and maybe a few robots.

— GARRET WESTLAKE, executive director, Virginia Commonwealth University, da Vinci Center for Innovation

Bill Bishop's latest book, *Dancing with Robots,* is an invitation to explore his 29 strategies for success in the New Economy. Entrepreneurs will find Bill's insights regarding the impact of AI on our future business models exciting and thought-provoking. Get your invitation to the dance now. I highly recommend it.

— PATRICK POWER, creator and founder of The Discovery Connection Program, discoverlistenconnect.com

Bill brings the reader into the future with *Dancing with Robots* and prepares the astute leader to shed old-world economy beliefs and, with urgency, learn, embrace, and put into practice New Economy beliefs. Why is this important? *The future has arrived* and many of us are asleep to the new reality of New Economy leadership essentials.

— KEITH CUPP, founder, Gravitas Impact

Dancing with Robots is another amazing futuristic book from Bill Bishop. After reading this book you will have an opportunity to become an industry transformer and be in that 10 percent of companies that embrace technology in order to survive, grow, and disrupt their industry.

— JEFFREY CALIBABA, CEO, SAPEL Inc.

DANCING
WITH
ROBOTS

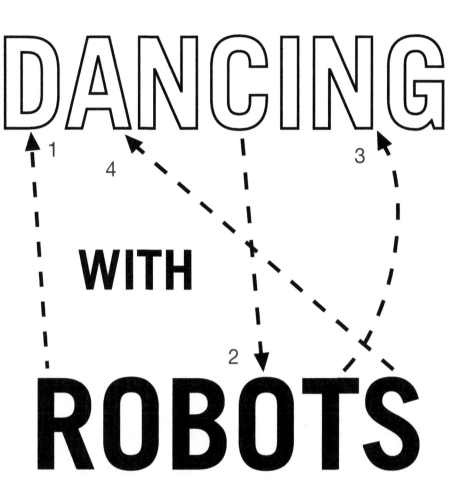

DANCING

WITH

ROBOTS

THE 29 STRATEGIES FOR SUCCESS
IN THE AGE OF AI AND AUTOMATION

BILL BISHOP

DUNDURN
PRESS

Publisher and Acquiring Editor: Scott Fraser | Editor: Michael Carroll
Cover designer: David Drummond

Library and Archives Canada Cataloguing in Publication

Title: Dancing with robots : the 29 strategies for success in the age of AI and automation / Bill Bishop.
Names: Bishop, Bill, 1957- author.
Description: Includes bibliographical references.
Identifiers: Canadiana (print) 20210352507 | Canadiana (ebook) 20210352590 | ISBN 9781459749023 (softcover) | ISBN 9781459749030 (PDF) | ISBN 9781459749047 (EPUB)
Subjects: LCSH: Technological innovations. | LCSH: Artificial intelligence. | LCSH: Automation.
Classification: LCC HD45 .B57 2022 | DDC 658.5/14—dc23

We acknowledge the support of the Canada Council for the Arts and the Ontario Arts Council for our publishing program. We also acknowledge the financial support of the Government of Ontario, through the Ontario Book Publishing Tax Credit and Ontario Creates, and the Government of Canada.

Care has been taken to trace the ownership of copyright material used in this book. The author and the publisher welcome any information enabling them to rectify any references or credits in subsequent editions.

The publisher is not responsible for websites or their content unless they are owned by the publisher.

Printed and bound in Canada.

Dundurn Press
1382 Queen Street East
Toronto, Ontario, Canada M4L 1C9
dundurn.com, @dundurnpress 𝕏 f ⌾

For Piper

Sooner or later, the U.S. will face mounting job losses due to advances in automation, artificial intelligence, and robotics.

— Oren Etzioni

As more and more artificial intelligence enters the world, more and more emotional intelligence must enter into leadership.

— Amit Ray

I do think, in time, people will have, sort of, relationships with certain kinds of robots — not every robot, but certain kinds of robots — where we feel that it is a sort of friendship, but it's going to be a robot-human kind.

— Cynthia Breazeal

It's not that we use technology, we live technology.

— Godfrey Reggio, American Director

There is an endless number of things to discover about robotics. A lot of it is just too fantastical for people to believe.

— Daniel W. Wilson

It has become appallingly obvious that our technology has exceeded our humanity.

— Albert Einstein

Thousands upon thousands have studied disease. Almost no one has studied health.

— Adelle Davis

One machine can do the work of fifty ordinary people. No machine can do the work of one extraordinary person.

— Elbert Hubbard

AI is good at describing the world as it is today with all of its biases, but it does not know how the world should be.

— Joanne Chen

Artificial intelligence is likely to be either the best or worst thing to happen to humanity.

— Stephen Hawking

Humans should be worried about the threat posed by artificial intelligence.

— Bill Gates

Machine intelligence is the last invention that humanity will ever need to make.

— Nick Bostrom

A robot may not injure a human being, or, through inaction, allow a human being to come to harm.

— Isaac Asimov

In the 21st century, the robot will take the place which slave labor occupied in ancient civilization.

— Nikola Tesla

We're going to become caretakers for the robots. That's what the next generation of work is going to be.

— Gray Scott

In the future, all robots will act like Don Knotts.

— Cesar Romero

I would like to die on Mars — just not on impact.

— Elon Musk

The future depends on what we do in the present.

— Mahatma Gandhi

CONTENTS

PREFACE

IT WILL BE the best of times, it will be the worst of times, it will be the age of wisdom or the age of foolishness. It will be the epoch of truth or the epoch of lies. It will be a season of light or a season of darkness. It will be the spring of hope or the spring of despair. We have everything before us or nothing before us. We're all going directly to heaven or we're all going the other way.

I paraphrase the first paragraph of *A Tale of Two Cities*, Charles Dickens's novel set against the backdrop of the French Revolution, because we find ourselves at a similar revolutionary juncture. Bloody and chaotic, the French Revolution not only changed France, it changed the world. Today, new revolutionary forces are stirring, driven by rapid advances in technology, and like it or not, the world will never be the same. The questions are: What will that future look like? What kind of dance will we have with robots?

I foresee two scenarios — one bright, the other dark. Which future we realize will depend on the choices we make today. We must forge the future we want and not accept one by default.

Let's start with the bright future. In this future, we skillfully navigate three realities of the New Economy: connectivity, super-intelligence, and dematerialization.

In the bright future, institutions are based on science, not superstition. Its core cultural project is to increase well-being using fewer resources. Its ethical foundations are openness, inclusion, equality, and democracy. The denizens of this future use technology to transcend rather than dominate, to help rather than harm, and to share rather than accumulate. Everyone benefits from technology. Everyone becomes more prosperous while rebalancing our relationship with nature.

In the bright future, we're increasingly interconnected. We can connect easily with every person on the planet, even the moon or Mars. We connect effortlessly with an ever-growing network of machines, devices, and robots from which we gather an exponentially increasing amount of data. We have our fingers on the pulse of the universe.

Superintelligent robots review this raging river of data and glean insights. The number one job of the robots is dematerialization. They help us get better results using fewer resources. As such, we don't extract as many resources from the earth while increasing prosperity.

Most of the value created in this bright future is intangible. Most of the tangible things we used to own, use, or see around us vanish.

The number one human job is to help one another successfully navigate change. We help our customers anticipate change and respond to change. We bring together our unique human amalgam of skills, talents, and abilities to identify and solve emergent problems. We also forge forward to achieve big ideas, solutions, and innovations that new technology makes possible.

Freed by the robots from manual labour and repetitive low-value symbol work, we think, dream, and care. We have more time for creative pursuits. We slow down and relax.

Traditional borders, boundaries, and categories become irrelevant. Nations of connection replace nation-states. The divisions between industrial sectors blur and disappear. The division of labour becomes irrelevant.

Living in a network, we see more readily how everything is connected. We see more clearly what connects us rather than divides us. Our incentive is to create more connections.

Robots are our servants, not our masters. Robots help us solve human problems, not robot problems, to achieve human goals, not robot goals.

We're no longer storehousers. We're conduits. Instead of gathering, accumulating, and protecting, we explore, curate, and share.

We're producers and consumers — prosumers. We simultaneously create value and consume value. We consume energy and create energy. We consume data and create data. We entertain and are entertained. We care and are cared for.

We replace *or* with *and*. We replace subtraction with addition, division with multiplication. We're additive rather than subtractive.

In this bright future, individuals own their means of data production. People know the value of their data and receive compensation for it. They understand that data is the most valuable currency of the New Economy. They also have complete control over their privacy and can calibrate exactly how much data they want to provide and sell.

The power structure of the network is distributed, not concentrated. The monopolistic data concentrators of the early internet have been replaced by the collective. Data, data storage, software, and processing power are spread across the network.

In the battle of good and evil, good prevails 51 percent of the time, gradually inching forward the moral arc of the universe. This epic battle is played out increasingly on the network, rather than on real-world battlefields. Good ideas and the truth overcome bad ideas and fake news like antibodies fighting malignant viruses.

In this bright future, we take a human-first approach. Humans first, robots second. Maybe even better, biology first, machines second.

Our key objective is health and happiness — well-being. If a robot or a machine helps us become healthier and happier, great. But if it makes us sicker and unhappier, not so good. We're vigilant and honest about the effects of technology and always equip our robots with an on-off switch.

What about the dark future?

Beyond the robotic dystopian tropes found in sci-fi movies like *The Matrix* and *The Terminator*, where the robots battle and enslave us, what's the realistic worst-case scenario?

In the dark future, robots are our masters. They tell us what to do. They make suggestions, and most of the time we act on those recommendations.

(This slide into servitude is already under way. The navigator in our cars tells us where to drive. Algorithms on Amazon suggest/tell us what to buy, and algorithms on social media/news sites tell us what to think, specifically, what to think about.)

In the dark future, artificial intelligence (AI) robots will give us a continuous stream of instructions about our health — exercise now! About our finances — buy now! And about our relationships — call our mothers-in-law now! At first, this guidance is welcome, but it doesn't take long before we lose agency and simply take orders.

Robots could also turn us into superhumans, exponentially increasing our physical and mental capacities. This might sound good, but it's likely the rich and privileged who will get these capacities first, giving them an insurmountable lead over the digital proletariat. We could end up with two classes of humans: a small coterie of robot-enriched ones lording it over the rest of us. A robotocracy. (This kind of inequity is already manifest. People living and working in high-bandwidth urban centres have a significant competitive advantage over folks in low-bandwidth rural regions.)

Dictators and autocrats could use technology to run a surveillance state. Employing data-mining, machine learning, surveillance cameras, tracking devices, and facial recognition, control-crazed leaders could keep tabs on their citizenry. They could use this information to clamp down on dissent and enforce social and economic behaviour. They'll know who we are, where we go, and what we do every minute of the day. They'll know how we feel and what we think. It will make Big Brother look like a small sibling by comparison.

Employers could use robots for nefarious ends. They can replace human employees with robots and have a big incentive to do that. But they can also use robots to track and control in minute detail the performance and behaviour of employees. They can monitor when they take a break or go to the washroom. They can use algorithms to rate their performance, determine compensation, and fire them if necessary. Taken to an extreme, they can employ robots to extract the maximum effort from their employees while minimizing the cost of labour. That's why it's important to recognize that robots don't just replace humans in the workplace; they can be used to dehumanize and exploit employees. It all depends on the intentions of the employer.

Millions of workers around the world could be thrown out of work by robots, not just blue-collar ones but in every profession, including lawyers, doctors, actors, writers, engineers, and computer programmers. As machine learning algorithms learn how to learn at an even faster clip, there's not much they couldn't do. Not only will they get smarter, they can also create more adroit robots that can do precision manual work — from picking tomatoes to performing eye surgery.

Robots will be able to write novels, compose music, and paint watercolour landscapes. They'll serve as nurses, truck drivers, electricians, and pilots, all of which will be highly disruptive. People will lose their jobs and incomes. They won't have anything to do. And in this dark future, the superhumans controlling everything won't care. They'll simply enlist guard robots to keep the dispossessed away from their yachts and gated compounds.

In the dark future, robots will be utilized to further exploit our natural resources — to pull more out of the earth and stimulate increased consumption. Instead of fostering a more balanced relationship with nature, faster and more powerful robots will give us greater dominion over it, thereby further destroying the environment.

In this future, robots take over the show. Every day they get smarter, faster, and more powerful. At first we think we can control them, but eventually they control us. Then we don't even understand what they're doing or how they're doing it. We become spectators, and then victims.

Frankly, the dark future is more likely because humans aren't great at dealing proactively with potential problems. We tend to hope for the best, that our profligacies won't have downsides, and if they do, we believe we can deal with it then. That's like smoking two packs of cigarettes a day with the backup plan that chemotherapy will save us if we get lung cancer.

Our current dance with robots is like riding a wild tiger. We hope we can hang on and won't fall off and get eaten by the tiger.

That's why we must think deeply about our relationship with robots. Do we want to have a functional or dysfunctional relationship? What will this relationship look like at every level — personally, in our careers, in our business, and in our society?

We must ask, what future do we want — the bright one or the dark one? Surely, we want the bright future, but we'll have to work on it. The robots are working on their future. They never sleep. So we need to wake up and get going.

In his 1952 novel, *Player Piano*, Kurt Vonnegut imagined a world where factories are run by robots and most people are unemployed and destitute. His novel posed important questions: What happens when robots take over human jobs? What do the unemployed humans do for work? How does the economy function if people without jobs can't afford to buy the products produced by robots? And most important: Is this the kind of world we want to live in?

As a 12-year-old science fiction buff, I read *Player Piano* with great interest. It was the first sci-fi novel I'd read that talked about economics, and it left a big impression on me. Its dystopian prophecy seemed plausible because companies have a compelling incentive to get rid of workers and automate their operations.

I realize now, however, that Vonnegut's book didn't go far enough. He only imagined the automation of manufacturing. He didn't predict a world where *everything* is automated — not just low-level manufacturing jobs but every kind of work, even the most advanced jobs. He didn't foresee the global internet, quantum computing, artificial intelligence, big data, machine learning algorithms, or the blockchain. He didn't predict a world where even the owners of factories can be disrupted and thrown into the street.

But that's the possible world emerging today. We live in an age where the piano doesn't need a player or a songwriter or even an audience. It's a world where the pianos manufacture themselves and then play their own compositions for one another. No humans necessary.

It's also a world where any company, organization, or institution can be displaced in a nanoflash. It's not simply a matter of taking an old business and adding robots to it. The core value proposition and competitive advantage of every old-style business could be upended by new kinds of fast-emerging competitors, disruptive technology, and topsy-turvy marketplace dynamics.

It's also a world that changes quickly. As the primary means of production shifts from a linear assembly-line structure to a networked value-hub configuration (see my book *The New Factory Thinker*), we're witnessing a concurrent realignment of the political and cultural composition of our society. New forms of political organizations, new types of money, and new ways of living are coming. Everything will change, and we need to be ready to deal with these changes.

Unfortunately, not everyone is awake to what's happening.

Since the release of *The New Factory Thinker*, I've given hundreds of speeches about the New Economy. From this experience, I've noticed that people relate to this subject in three distinct ways.

About 10 percent of the people I meet are enthusiastic about the topic. They're excited about the future. They're eager to create a New Economy business or career.

Sixty percent are zoned out. They think the New Economy and technology like artificial intelligence and the blockchain won't affect them.

The remaining 30 percent are angry. They're threatened by the New Economy and sometimes blame me for broaching the subject. I've had numerous people hurl insults at me and then stomp out of my speeches. (Don't worry; I'm used to it.)

After speaking to more than 20,000 people at live events, I've concluded that 90 percent of the population isn't prepared for what's coming. They're either oblivious to their predicament or angry about it and have no plan for the future. This cohort includes political leaders. Just a handful appreciate the massive shift that's taking place, a shift that will render obsolete most of the jobs humans hold today. Most of these disrupted people will be thrown into the street with nothing to do (as in *Player Piano*). Others will find something new to do. Sadly, few of our leaders are thinking about what these new "jobs" might be.

One suggestion is a minimum monthly income. The idea is to tax companies that use robots and then give the proceeds to the "disrupted." And while it sounds well intentioned and might be a temporary fix, I think the idea is misguided. One, the companies targeted by the tax will figure out a way to avoid it. It will also be hard to determine which robots to tax. Can an algorithm or a quantum computer processor on the cloud be taxed? Imagine the endless negotiations. But more importantly, the minimum-income idea is a lazy answer to what I call "The Player Piano Problem." Better to figure out new kinds of work for people to do rather than simply pay them not to work. I believe most people want and need meaningful employment.

The challenges we face are daunting but not unprecedented. At the beginning of the 20th century, most people worked in agriculture. Today, only a small percentage of people work on farms. A century ago, our ancestors would have been dumbfounded had they known that people in the future would work as app designers, social media managers, mindfulness teachers, or Airbnb hosts. Not to mention system engineers, data analysts, theme park entertainers, or virtual world designers. People back then thought the end of farm jobs meant the end of good jobs. The exact opposite happened.

The fact is that new technology and its impact can be painful for the people being disrupted. But the New Economy will also bring forth new opportunities for wonderful and previously unimaginable work. Mark my words, in the New Economy, people will make money in ways we can't fathom right now. Our kids will have careers we won't understand. (My mother-in-law doesn't have a clue what I do. When told I run The BIG Idea Company, she looks perplexed and horrified. Lawyer or accountant is a more acceptable son-in-law occupation.)

To succeed in the New Economy, we need to learn how to "dance" with robots. We won't be able to beat them, and we can't ignore them. We need to learn how to embrace and dance gracefully with them — to create something beautiful together.

So let's take some dance lessons.

First, I prognosticate two future scenarios — a bright future and a dark future — so we all recognize the stakes involved. Then, I explore the Five Human Superpowers we can bring to the dance:

1. Embodied Pattern Recognition
2. Unbridled Curiosity
3. Purpose-Driven Ideation
4. Ethical Framing
5. Metaphoric Communication

Next, I outline The 29 Strategies for Success in the Age of AI and Automation. These principles give you a roadmap to confidently navigate this new reality. For example, we look at the core incentive driving the New Economy (Strategy No. 1: Increase Well-Being Using Fewer Resources) in contrast to the core incentive that drove the old economy (more consumption equals happiness). Strategy No. 1 makes the case that old deeply conditioned patterns of thinking are the biggest roadblocks to success in the New Economy and then provides alternative ways of thinking that are more effective.

Then a powerful step-by-step method for dancing with robots is delineated, a method that provides a path to follow that's future-proof, scalable, and uplifting. It empowers us to bring all our heart and soul into our lives and work and is based on The BIG Idea Adventure, my coaching program.

Humans are interesting creatures. On the one hand, we're quite good at living in delusion. We can blindly ignore impending catastrophes until they hit us square in the face. On the other hand, we're incredible at confronting challenges once the battle is upon us. My mission is to wake people up to "The Player Piano Problem" and help them dance to a new tune, one they write and perform themselves (with a little help from robots).

Ready to join the dance? If so, let the music begin.

INTRODUCTION

The Five Human Superpowers

DANCING WITH ROBOTS isn't a physical activity. To dance with robots, we bring our intellect, creativity, and moral compass to the dance floor. But first, we need to get acquainted with our partner.

Every passing day, robots — actual robots, but also other technology such as AI, nanotechnology, the Internet of Things (IoT), and quantum computing — will become faster, smarter, and more capable. They'll also be ubiquitous, finding their way into every aspect of our lives until they become invisible and we forget they're even there. We'll have a relationship with them, and like all relationships, it will either be functional, dysfunctional, or somewhere in between.

I like to think I have a functional relationship with my Google Navigator. It's an integral part of my life. I use it every time I drive, even on short trips. I rely on it to tell me the best route. I don't think about how remarkable it is anymore, in the same way I don't marvel at the refrigerator every time I'm in the kitchen.

My dance with Google Navigator has been going on for many years. I've learned to listen when it tells me to take a different route or exit the highway unexpectedly. I've developed faith that it knows things I don't and that it has my best interests at heart. I even feel guilty when I don't obey its suggestions, wondering if it will penalize me at some future date for my lack of compliance.

Using Google Navigator has made business trips more relaxing because I know, even while stuck in traffic, that I'll arrive at my meeting on time. I think it's a wonderful invention, even though I know it's gathering data about me — analyzing where I go and what I do.

But recently, I've come to wonder where technology like Google Navigator is taking us. I'm fortunate to own a rustic log home about three hours north of Toronto where I often retreat to ponder the universe. When my wife, Ginny, and I first bought the place, I was annoyed to discover that lots of cars and trucks used our road, often despoiling the quiet solitude. But these days hardly anyone takes our road. Besides the odd car, the only traffic is horse-drawn carriages driven by our Amish neighbours.

I didn't think about why the traffic disappeared until the other day when I used Google Navigator for my trip home to Toronto. It instructed me to follow a much different route than I'd taken for the previous 20 years. It said I'd knock 30 minutes off the trip. No longer three hours, but two and a half hours.

Along the way, I noticed that a stream of cars took the same back road I was on, both coming and going. Serious traffic. It then dawned on me that everyone was on the same road because Google Navigator was giving them the same instructions. I also realized that drivers weren't taking my road anymore because Google didn't direct them there.

That's great for me but not so great for the people on the busy road. They probably wonder why hundreds of cars now barrel down their previously sleepy byway. I also speculated that my road had been forsaken because it features a small (but scenic) bend around a small lake. The Google algorithm probably calculates that the bend in the road adds a few seconds to the trip, and so it nixed our road.

The implications of this situation are far-reaching. First, what if the people on the now-busy road don't like the increased traffic? What can they do about it? They can't call the local government. The government has no power over Google. The people on the road can't call Google, either. The company isn't in the business of changing its algorithm to accommodate a few disgruntled ratepayers. So the people on the busy road have been disenfranchised by an algorithm.

Second, I realized the new route didn't take me to Super Burgers, my favourite halfway rest stop. If I follow Google's advice, there are no more delicious cheeseburgers for me. But more significant than the effect on my deprived tastebuds, Super Burgers has lost a customer because of an algorithm, and if it loses enough customers, it might go out of business. Even more alarming, it won't know why it lost customers and will have no way to rectify the situation.

Third, what happens when we just take orders from Google Navigator and other similar AI-driven apps? Will we be human beings anymore, or simply automatons following the dictates of a digital overlord? It reminds me of the old *Flash Gordon* movie serial from the 1930s where the evil emperor enslaved the population by getting people to wear brainwashing helmets. (Check it out on YouTube.) If we stay on the same trajectory and mindlessly bring AI into all areas of our lives, won't it just tell us what to do all day long? Get up. Make bed. Brush teeth. Floss. Eat yogurt. Go to work.

In my 1996 book, *Strategic Marketing for the Digital Age* (the first book in the world about internet marketing, by the way), I introduced a concept called "Technopia." When we're infected by Technopia, we adopt technology with little regard for potential negative repercussions that might result unexpectedly. We absolve ourselves of any moral or ethical implications associated with our technological infatuations. We see all new technology as a good.

Of course, we've seen that technology isn't always a good thing. Everything in life seems to have both an upside and a downside. Technology is no exception. Most people never imagined all the negative repercussions caused by the internet and social media.

Today, Technopia is rampant. Dozens of new technologies are ascending, and little caution is being exercised. These technologies include machine learning algorithms (think of them as robots that keep getting smarter), big-data analytics (the robots know a lot about us), the IoT (the robots have many ways to spy on us and gather data), and nanotechnology (the robots are getting smaller and smaller). Not to mention drones (robots that fly), quantum computing (robots with unlimited processing power), and the blockchain (robots conducting high-speed transactions with each other). As these technologies advance exponentially, is anyone taking precautions to ensure the outcomes are beneficial to humans?

That's why our human-robot relationship is a dance. We can sit out the dance and become techno-wallflowers, or we can dance with every robot that comes along. Or we can learn to embrace our robot partners in a skillful, even elegant, way that makes the world a better place. We can also decide which robots we want invited to the dance.

It's not unreasonable to fear the rise of robots. They can do a lot of things better and faster than humans. If we run a business, we have a strong incentive to replace humans with automation. Robots can complete repetitive tasks faster and more efficiently. They can operate 24/7, never take a break, never call in sick, and never go on strike. They also keep learning how to do their job faster and better. It's not a stretch to predict that millions of jobs will be lost to automation in the coming decade.

Faced with this problem, humans have a trait that's not helpful. It's called the *status quo bias*. Even though we can see that things have changed dramatically in the past, we tend to think the future will be more or less the same as the present (perhaps with jetpacks and flying cars). We can't imagine the future might be radically different, so we don't prepare for it.

The *status quo bias* is exacerbated by the way our brains are wired. Our brains are currently configured for the Industrial Revolution. Over the past 250 years, our thinking patterns have mirrored the assembly-line nature of how we organized our economy. Because our survival depended on how well we fit into this linear industrial framework, our brains were formed to think in a linear, step-by-step fashion. We then designed our society to mirror this means of production (assembly lines), which then further reinforced the industrial pathways in our brains. I'm certainly not a neuroscientist, but once I developed this hypothesis, it became clear to me that most of us (99 percent) are what I call "old factory thinkers." It's been my mission for the past several years to explain this concept and elucidate why old factory thinking is obsolete and no longer helpful in the New Economy.

If we've been flabbergasted by the roller-coaster political and economic upheavals of the past few years, we can attribute them to one major cause: the global transition from the old economy to the New Economy, from an economy predicated on assembly lines and assembly-line thinking to an economy structured as a network. This is a historic and unprecedented shift that few people understand or acknowledge.

There's a helpful way to understand this shift. For the past 250 years, we went to work in a physical place: a farm, a factory, an office, or a store. (Hospitals, schools, and other forms of physical workplaces can be added.) In these locales, we were part of an assembly line. We received inputs from upstream, added value by doing our task, and then passed our work downstream. To excel in the assembly line, we needed to be focused, fast, and single-minded. Our primary contribution was to keep the assembly line moving.

I experienced this role first-hand when I worked on an assembly line in a brewery for two summers in my early twenties. While I got to drink a lot of beer (the core feature of the benefits plan), the work was tedious and stressful. My biggest nightmare was that I would do something that caused my bottle-packing machine to jam thereby bringing the entire factory to a halt.

Now you might say you don't work on an assembly line. You're a doctor, a lawyer, an IT professional, or an entrepreneur. You don't work in a brewery. But the fact is, you still work on an assembly line. How your work is organized, and how you think about your work, is structured as an assembly line. The problem is that this way of thinking is so commonplace that we don't see that it's actually a *way* of thinking. It's just our reality.

But something changed. Although we might still go to work in an office, a home office, a factory, or a farm (my son is an organic farmer), we actually go to work somewhere else these days. We all go to work in a network, and that network is called the internet. Every day more and more of our activities are conducted on this network, and that changes everything.

It changes everything because the skills, attitudes, and ways of being needed to thrive on an assembly line aren't the ones needed to succeed in a network. It's as if we show up at a swimming pool with our hockey skates.

Let me give you some examples.

15

On the assembly line, the job is to focus on the task at hand. Don't look left. Don't look right. Don't look up or down. Eyes and body kept forward.

On the assembly line, we're not encouraged to engage in conversations with our co-workers. That just slows things down and might be perceived as union organizing.

On the assembly line, we don't think much about what we're actually building, what the end result will be (unless it's something personally important like beer!). We just do our parts of the job for eight hours and go home.

On the assembly line, we don't think much about the ethical or moral implications of what we're doing. The only good is production and consumption. We're not encouraged to question the wider or longer-term implications of our livelihoods.

On the assembly line, creativity is discouraged. No one wants us to do our jobs in new and novel ways. That might screw things up.

Now you might say I'm being extreme in this characterization of life on the assembly line, but I disagree. To a certain degree, we've all made this bargain with the assembly-line economy. It's a matter of survival.

Now let's consider what it means to work in a network. What are the skills, attitudes, and ways of being that work in that environment?

First, it's important to realize that the network I refer to isn't first and foremost a technology. It's actually a network of relationships mediated by technology. People connected to people. People connected to robots. Robots connected to robots.

In this environment, we need to bring our swimsuits to the pool, not our hockey skates. We need to learn how to swim, not skate.

In a network, we need to look around, to the left, to the right, up and down, and inside out. We need to constantly stay abreast about what's happening in the network. Who are the people and robots in our networks? What are they doing? What are they thinking? How do they perceive us? What does the network want? What is it asking of us?

In a network, we don't think in a linear fashion. We think spatially. We gather information from manifold, seemingly unrelated sources. These sources include not just the digital but analogue, using our five physical senses, plus mindful attention to our internal moods, thought patterns, perceptions, and conditioned biases. We then use this data to identify previously unseen patterns. This activity is called "embodied pattern recognition."

In a network, curiosity is an extremely desirable trait. We're endlessly interested in the world around us. No realm of the world or the imagination is off limits. Ever curious, we ask ourselves, other people, and robots deep, meaningful questions. This is called "unbridled curiosity."

To prosper in a network, we provide lots of ideas. By recognizing patterns, we put forward ideas to do things better, solve problems, and achieve goals. Most importantly, our ideas have purposes — to help others. This is called "purpose-driven ideation."

To maintain and grow our networks, we're clear and overt about the ethical principles that guide our thoughts, actions, and speech. We're cognizant of the ultimate outcomes of our livelihoods and act accordingly. We're aware that our ethical reputations are key elements of our network statuses and successes. This is called "ethical framing."

In a networked world that's inherently complex and ever-changing, we know that influence and action are prefaced by skillful communication. To lead and provide value in our networks, we clearly explain our aspirations, our ideas, our ethical principles, and our roles. We tell stories using metaphors, analogies, and strong narratives that capture the imagination of the people in our networks. This is called "metaphoric communication."

These five attributes — embodied pattern recognition, unbridled curiosity, purpose-driven ideation, ethical framing, and metaphoric communication — serve two purposes. One, they help us thrive in a network of people and robots. Two, they help humans provide value that can't be delivered by robots.

They are our Human Superpowers.

Unlike robots, we have bodies. Our bodies have sensory inputs that robots don't have. This enables us to pick up patterns robots can't see. As innately curious creatures, we can pursue paths of inquiry that transcend robots, especially if we partner with them in this inquiry. While robots are great at learning and carrying out tasks with alacrity, humans are inherently good at coming up with inventive ideas, especially if they're driven by higher purposes. Moreover, as humans, we can bring an ethical perspective to the dance to ensure the project or undertaking will produce a common good. And finally, metaphorical thinking and storytelling are uniquely human qualities robots don't possess, at least not yet.

As we can see, living and working in a network is significantly different compared to living and working on an assembly line. The skills that served us well for 250 years are obsolete and can be better done by robots. In fact, these old skills are impediments. If we work in a network (we all do now) but behave as if it's an assembly line, the network won't reward us. The transition to the new networked economy is upending the old order. The power brokers of the old economy have mounted a spirited but ultimately doomed defence of the status quo. Their efforts are doomed because the network is now the new means of production. Inexorably, those who embrace the network will prosper. Those who reject it will perish. It's actually that stark.

The truth of my declaration — that old factory thinkers will perish and new factory thinkers will ascend — will become even more apparent as we delve into The 29 Strategies for Success in the Age of AI and Automation.

The way we need to think about business and the economy needs to change on a fundamental level. The Industrial Revolution is receding in the rearview mirror. The New Economy is ahead of us. So let's explore it.

THE

STRATEGIES FOR SUCCESS

IN THE AGE OF AI AND AUTOMATION

STRATEGY NO. 1

Increase Well-Being Using Fewer Resources

EVERY CULTURE HAS a master project. The project pursued by ancient Athenians was to create a democracy of equals (unless you were a woman, slave, or poor person). In Europe during the Middle Ages, the project was the Christian Crusades (let's go and kill the heretics). In revolutionary Bolshevik Russia, the project was to create a communist paradise of the proletariat as envisioned by Karl Marx (didn't quite work out that way).

The cultural project gives the tribe, nation, or race a historical trajectory and purpose, even though the project itself might not be overtly communicated. It informs and directs the decisions made by the culture's community. This cultural project is also based on a formula for success, once again rarely communicated directly or generally acknowledged. In Nazi Germany, the formula was *racial purity equals greatness*. In ancient Rome, the formula was *bigger empire equals greater power*. In Oliver Cromwell's Puritan England, the formula was *anti-papist piety equals spiritual salvation*.

In the Western world since the dawn of the Industrial Revolution in the late 18th century, the cultural project has been to generate economic growth through the expansion of production and consumption. The formula for success driving this project was *greater consumption equals greater happiness*. Every participant in this culture was raised on this mother's milk. Our parents, teachers, celebrities, media personalities, and political leaders have exhorted us to consume more, and by extension, produce more.

Bear in mind, I'm not judging this formula for success as good or bad; I'm just pointing out that we've been using a formula for success to achieve a cultural project. There's no arguing that this project has been successful. Billions of people around the world have been raised out of poverty. This formula has helped eradicate many diseases and foster greater equality and social justice (still a work in progress, of course). But it's also folly to argue that this formula hasn't produced its share of problems: environmental degradation, species extinction, nihilistic materialism, systemic inequality, and endemic racism. What I'm arguing is that this cultural project and its underlying success formula is now obsolete and not conducive to economic and personal success in the New Economy.

Using the equation *greater consumption equals greater happiness* is obsolete because the network marketplace mandates something else. It demands and selects products and services that serve another equation: *increase well-being using fewer resources*. Companies, organizations, individuals — and robots — that observe this equation are in high demand. (Note: the equation could also be stated as achieve a better result using fewer resources. However, the ultimate result is well-being, so it eventually points to that beneficial peak outcome.)

There are plenty of examples of this formula already being rewarded in the New Economy marketplace. Let's start with Google Navigator. Its raison d'être is to help achieve a better result using fewer resources: get to a destination using less time and energy. Airbnb helps book a room, home, or even a treehouse easily while generating new kinds of revenue for hosts. Grocery Gateway, a Canadian grocery-delivery service, helps its customers spend more time doing what they love and less time and energy driving to and from the grocery store. Local tool libraries help their members get construction projects done by lending out tools for an annual fee. People no longer need to buy tools or even rent them. They can be taken out and returned just like books from libraries. Once again, increasing well-being using fewer resources.

Now it might seem that I'm promoting an environmental green lefty agenda that will undermine economic growth and lead to a totalitarian socialist nightmare, but far from it. I'm an ardent entrepreneur with a pro-business agenda. My conjecture is that this New Economy formula is great for business. In fact, it's the only viable formula for success going forward. Why? Because consumers will reward products or services that help them get a better result (well-being) using fewer resources. If a way is shown to save on energy bills (using LED light bulbs and a smart thermostat, for example), people are inclined to buy them. If an electric- or hydrogen-powered car is demonstrated to be 50 percent less expensive to operate and maintain, we're inclined to buy it. If there's an app-for-anything or platform-for-anything that gets better results for less time, money, energy, or effort, we're all over it.

It sounds obvious that this formula is a winner for any company to pursue, but our old factory thinking gets in the way. In the old economy, we wanted customers to consume more because we thought that was the only way to make money. *More consumption equals more money.* But that's not true in the New Economy. If your competitor offers your customer a better result using fewer resources, your customers will drop you in an instant.

As I explained in *The New Factory Thinker*, the old formula puts us at odds with customers because our incentives don't align with their incentives. If we want our customers to consume more, and they want to consume less, that's a fundamental disconnect. But if our incentives are aligned (we help them get a better result using fewer resources), then market success is more likely. But to get there, we have to eschew the old economy formula and embrace the new one.

This is the first strategy for success in the New Economy because it's the overriding principle that underpins all other strategies. All of them point back to this strategy.

Observing economic and business trends through this lens is a helpful way to reinforce this strategy in our minds. It's my prognostication that this new success formula will completely transform our economy and then our society. As more entities serve this new cultural project, the changes will accelerate.

Such a transformation will be driven by robots, especially AI, whose principal task, if we think about it for a second, is to help achieve a better result utilizing fewer resources. As machine learning AIs become smarter and faster, they'll constantly look for ways to wrest better results out of our physical world employing fewer and fewer resources. That's why we might see that fossil fuels and other earthbound resources are no longer needed in the quantities we consume them now (a process is called dematerialization). The price of oil might fall dramatically. We might see that money isn't needed as much as it used to be, leading to negative interest rates where a bank pays us to borrow money and charges us to deposit it in its vault. Every day there will be new ways to get better results using fewer resources. While these changes will be imperceptible on a daily basis, the *drip-drip-drip* of these changes will eventually result in an oceanic change in how we live. That's why I'm so bullish on the future, because economic incentives now point to well-being rather than increased consumption, promising a more sustainable future.

With regard to this fundamental principle, human beings play a key role in the dance with robots. While robots will get better at achieving a better result utilizing fewer resources, human beings are needed to ensure these efforts actually produce greater well-being for people. If we ask robots to protect the earth from its enemies, they might turn their guns away from potential alien invaders and start eradicating humans because they consider the species hostile to the health of the planet. We have to make sure we don't fall into the trap of Technopia (all technology is good). We need to make sure our technological partners work toward well-being.

So our task is clear: start brainstorming. How can we help others achieve greater well-being using fewer resources? And while this might feel hard at first, if we persevere, we'll generate dozens of original ideas. Then the dance will truly begin.

STRATEGY NO. 2

Focus First on Who We Want to Help

THE FIRST FEW years of college are often more about having a good time than pursuing higher realms of learning. I can certainly attest to that. My early years in journalism were a party-fuelled whirlwind that's frankly hard to remember in great detail. But eventually we have to get our acts together and do what my friend Eddy used to say: "Sooner or later, you've got to wake up and smell the coffee."

So when my stepdaughter, Robin, woke up one morning in her twenties at university and smelled the coffee, a palpable degree of panic set in. "What am I going to do with my life and career?" she bemoaned one night around the dinner table. "There are so many things I could do and I just can't decide."

I remember asking the same questions when I was her age. I was perplexed because I didn't fit into any of the normal categories. I didn't want to be a lawyer, doctor, or journalist, even though the last was my major. It was scary and depressing not to have a direction, and I desperately believed I needed to choose one or I was going to live out of a dumpster. Never in my wildest imagination would I have guessed I'd be an entrepreneur running a business called The BIG Idea Company and write a book entitled *Dancing with Robots.*

In the old economy, choosing a career meant picking a skill, trade, or profession. It meant selecting an industry to work in and finding a role in that industry. Sometimes people fell into these roles by accident. Sometimes they were compelled by their parents. And sometimes they made decisions proactively on their own. Regardless of the circumstances, the principle was clear: to get focused meant to choose a trade or profession.

From the context of a company, the principle was the same. Each company was part of a particular industry and sold a specific product or service. The company or organization was defined by its product or service: we make pencils, we sell furniture, we clean houses, we sell insurance.

In the New Economy, this way of thinking is breaking down for two major reasons. One, when we build careers or businesses around a particular established product or service, we face lots of competition, which drives down how much income we can make. Simple supply and demand. Two, in a world that's constantly changing, it's foolish to build businesses or careers around something that might be rendered obsolete, either by new technology (robots), new kinds of competition, or changes in market conditions.

In addition, choosing a product or service specialty in the New Economy limits potential. In my mind, everyone has the potential to be a gourmet chef (providing premium-level products and services), but most people go to work every day and sell hot dogs (commodities). That's because there's already an industry in place for selling hot dogs. We just have to learn how to run a hot dog stand. But how many of us really want to sell hot dogs for 40 or 50 years?

Although this hot dog concept is an analogy, I actually did sell hot dogs one summer on the Toronto Islands when I was 16 years old. It entailed 10-hour days, and I got paid the grand sum of $1.65 per hour, the minimum wage at the time. It was boring and ultimately nauseating. When we're on the inside, we learn that hot dogs are truly odious, especially in 32°C-heat with high humidity.

That's why I'm so passionate about helping people become gourmet chefs. We can all do it, but there's one huge impediment. Unlike hot dog industries, there's no ready-made system out there for a unique gourmet business. We have to invent it. And most people don't know how. That's one reason my BIG Idea Company has been so enjoyable. We help people who are fed up selling hot dogs to create packages and systems to sell gourmet meals, and it's extremely gratifying to see their transformation. They're happier, more fulfilled, they make more money, and they work less. They're also in a much better position to prosper in the New Economy. Instead of being replaced by robots (who are great at running hot dog stands), they work in conjunction with robots to serve up one-of-a-kind, high-value gourmet meals.

So how do we get to this better place? Instead of choosing a particular product, service, skill, profession, or industry, decide instead who we want to help. Think about what kind of person, company, or organization we want to work with. For example, 20 years ago, I decided I wanted to help forward-thinking business people with good intentions. I didn't start by deciding what I wanted to make, sell, or deliver. I decided first with who I wanted to have business relationships for the rest of my working life.

Focusing first on who we want to help sounds so simple, yet it's actually quite difficult at first. It's difficult because our old factory brains are wired to first choose a product or service. We're also not wired to think about others; we're wired to think about ourselves. (That's not to say we're inherently selfish or self-centred; it's just that 200-plus years of industrial conditioning has wired our brains that way.) I notice this general trait when I talk to people about their businesses. They usually talk about their companies and rarely talk about their customers. It's all about them.

Focusing first on who we want to help makes everything much clearer and opens up an unimpeded path forward. It gives us a solid, immutable anchor that will stabilize our lives, careers, and businesses. If our businesses or careers are built around helping a particular type of person or organization, change, even the unpredictable kind, won't upend our strategic directions. In fact, change will be our ally because a key value we can provide in the New Economy is to help our customers deal effectively with change. And because change is an unlimited resource, we'll never run out of ways to help our target customers.

This leads to the key point of this New Economy strategy. When we pick our "customer types," we also adopt the attitude that we're prepared to help them any way we can. We're prepared to build a "value hub" around them, which means anything is possible. We're also willing to combine different "value components" to help our customers solve problems and achieve goals (more on value hubs and value components later).

If we start our thinking with who we want to help, we'll be better dance partners with robots. Instead of feeling threatened that robots will take over our hot dog stands, we'll look for ways to work with robots to cook up better gourmet meals for our customers.

This New Economy strategy also fosters greater well-being. Instead of getting caught up in the frenzied endeavour to sell more hot dogs, which might or might not be good for our mental or spiritual well-being, we focus instead on helping people. That's our first and foremost intention. It makes us feel better about ourselves and what we do for a living.

This New Economy strategy certainly helped my two kids. When my stepdaughter, Robin, had her wake-up-and-smell-the-coffee moment, I told her: "Instead of trying to figure out first what you want to do, figure out who you want to help." It didn't take her long to come up with an answer: "I want to help people who are less fortunate than us," she said. I told her to keep that thought front and centre when thinking about her career. She did. Over the years that followed, she completed her master's degree in social work and now has a great job working in a social services agency. She's gratified that she's doing meaningful and interesting work that helps people.

I also gave my son, Doug, the same advice. And today he and his life partner run an organic farm in Quebec near Ottawa. They've combined their knowledge and skills in organic farming, art, and marketing to build a thriving entrepreneurial enterprise.

To dance with robots, start by deciding who we want to help, not what we want to make, sell, or deliver. Begin there.

Who do we want to help?

STRATEGY NO. 3

Build a Value Proposition
Around a Big Idea

WE NEVER KNOW where we'll be born. When I was about six years old, my mother showed me my birth certificate. I was surprised that you needed a document to prove you were born. "Obviously, I was born," I said precociously. "Why would you need a piece of paper for that?"

My mom explained that the document certified I was a Canadian citizen born on April 5, 1957, in Edmonton, Alberta. Holding the birth certificate in my hand, I felt an odd sense of pride and personhood I'd never experienced before. But I was also surprised. "Where's Edmonton?" I asked. "We live in Toronto. Why was I born in Edmonton?"

It turned out my parents lived in Edmonton in the late 1950s because my father was sent there to open a branch office for Ronald Reynolds, an ad agency. That's the reason why the blessed historic event, my birth, took place in Edmonton and not Toronto. I thought that was cool but didn't realize my Edmonton lineage would come in handy many years later.

Being born in Edmonton is useful because I often find myself giving speeches and workshops in Alberta. Normally, a person from central

Canada, especially from Toronto, can expect a rough ride from an Albertan audience. There's a strain of anti-central-Canada animosity prevalent in Alberta that has deep roots in the history of the country. So it's dicey. But I have an ace up my sleeve. I preface my talk by revealing that I was actually born in Edmonton and therefore they can think of me as a fellow Albertan who has returned from the den of the devil otherwise known as Toronto. That usually gets a chuckle from the crowd.

My Albertan bona fides also give me permission to speak frankly about the Alberta economy, which, of course, is built around the oil and gas industry. In Alberta, there's really only one business: oil and gas. The fortunes of almost every sector of its economy are tied to the fortunes of oil, specifically the price of oil. When the price of oil goes up, people in Alberta are happy. When the price of oil goes down, everyone is sad or angry.

So what's Alberta got to do with this New Economy strategy: Build a Value Proposition Around a Big Idea? It's a cautionary tale about what can happen if we use the obverse old economy strategy: Build a Value Proposition Around a Product or Service.

For the past century, Alberta has structured its economy around the oil and gas industry. Over that time, the province's economy has grown exponentially. During the 1970s, Alberta had something called the Heritage Fund, which was meant to be a kind of oil-based trust fund for Albertans. Personally, I was counting on my share. Hey, here's my birth certificate! Unfortunately, I never got my share, nor did anyone else, because Alberta ran into trouble when oil prices collapsed suddenly and unexpectantly in 2014–15. The price of crude dropped from over $100 a barrel to under $25. Fortunately for Alberta, the price recovered (as of this writing), but it hasn't yet regained its previous stratospheric heights.

The key word in the previous paragraph is *unexpectantly*. Albertans never thought the price of oil was going to collapse. They had the *status quo bias*. In 2014, they thought the future would be much like the past. They envisioned the price of oil would continue to go up as the world supply of oil depleted. It was an understandable expectation, but an erroneous one. In today's New Economy, a key defining feature is unpredictable change. No matter what we think the future might hold, we're probably wrong. Did we think in 2000 that we'd be posting to Facebook, using our smartphones to order an Uber, or that Donald Trump would be elected president? Surely not. So we can be sure the coming decades will bring changes we never predicted. In all likelihood, something will probably happen in the next week that we weren't predicting. Think Covid-19.

Yet my fellow Albertans didn't see the oil price collapse coming. They didn't want to see it coming. They didn't want to think about the future and the potentially difficult changes it might bring. Who wants to think about that?

But here's the thing. We might not be interested in the future, but the future is interested in us. And the future was interested in Alberta. It was a wake-up call. Albertans were suddenly faced with the prospect of a much different future than they'd banked on. So much so that they themselves did something unpredictable. They elected a socialist provincial government after decades of conservative rule. That blew my mind. I didn't see that coming.

So let's get really clear. We can't predict the future. It probably won't look anything like the past or present. There are forces at play that we have absolutely no control over. Even if things are going peachy right now, it doesn't mean it's going to stay that way.

That's why this New Economy strategy is so important. It helps us future-proof our businesses, our careers, and even our lives. If we build our value proposition around a product or service like oil, we're likely to be trampled at some point. That's what happened to Research in Motion (RIM) and its BlackBerry product. It built its future around a hand-held device and went from a darling to disaster overnight when the iPhone came along. And because RIM was using old economy thinking, it couldn't pivot; its thinking got in the way. The same happened in Alberta, and it's still happening. I'll come back to that shortly.

To make ourselves future-proof in a world of chaotic change, the better approach is to anchor ourselves around a big idea, a core concept that isn't directly tied to, or dependent on, a particular product or service. This big idea gives us a direction and path that will be unimpeded no matter what happens. It also gives us the creative latitude to generate an infinite array of value components (or if the old economy appellations are preferred, products and services).

A big idea has three elements: *the big goal*, *the big problem*, and *the signature activity*. I'll explain them here in a linear fashion, but they can be considered in any order.

The big goal defines what we help our ideal customers achieve. It's not our goal; it's the aspiration we have for them. For example, we might want to help them become 10 times happier or 50 times healthier. We might want to help them become 25 times more successful or learn 15 times more quickly. Notice that I give each goal a quantitative measure like 15 or 50 times. The large number is deliberate. I encourage even saying 100 or 500 times. This approach supports a belief that big things are possible, something old factory thinking typically knocked out of us. The key is to remember that our big goal isn't a promise. We can't promise we'll make someone 12 times stronger, but we can make it our intention. An intention isn't the same as a promise.

The second element is the big problem. As I said, we can start here if we like. Using embodied pattern recognition, we're able to see problems afflicted people or organizations can't see. In my case, I could discern that companies were caught in old factory thinking, based on my work with thousands of firms. They couldn't see this problem, but I could. So my aspiration was and is to help people recognize how old factory thinking is holding them back and help them use new factory thinking to grow their businesses 10 times bigger and better.

Problems are an endless resource in the New Economy; we just have to look for them. When we're stuck on an assembly line, bosses don't want us to hunt for problems. They just want us to do our jobs. That's what happened when I worked at the brewery. No one noticed for six weeks that we were putting the wrong labels on beer bottles. We weren't supposed to look for problems. As such, the company lost millions. (The upside, however, was that the employees got to drink the erroneously labelled beer, which tasted the same regardless.)

But by using this New Economy strategy, our job is now to keep searching for problems to solve, and the great thing is we'll never run out of them. A good example is LifeLock. This company helps to protect identities from the attacks of online predators. Its value proposition is based on solving a big problem that didn't exist before the internet. There's another company called Reputation Defender that helps restore a good name when it's sullied by trolls on social media. These businesses are predicated on solving new kinds of problems that have arisen. That's why rapid change has a perverse benefit: it propagates problems. Every new technology and structural realignment produces unexpected issues. As we eagerly embrace new wonders, we usually find out later that they caused new problems. That's great for new factory thinkers like us because we'll never run out of problems to solve. (More on this topic with Strategy No. 18: Make Problems a Renewable Resource.)

The third element of a big idea is the signature activity. When we're willing to provide any kind of value to our customers (see Strategy No. 2), we still need to put forward a defining function to anchor our value proposition. For example, in my case, my signature activity is the big idea. (This is delightfully post-modern: my big idea is the big idea!) I realized in the 1990s that my most powerful defining function was to help people come up with innovative big ideas. I was good at it and loved doing it. So everything starts from there. My very first session with a prospect is called The BIG Idea Conversation. My membership program is called The BIG Idea Adventure, and my YouTube channel is called Bill Bishop's BIG Idea Show. Everything is about the big idea.

The thing I appreciate most about my value proposition is that it's future-proof. I can't imagine big ideas are going to become obsolete. In fact, I believe big ideas will become even more important in the future as people are forced to reinvent themselves. And if robots get good at creative brainstorming, I look forward to collaborating with them on big ideas. (I actually use robots now in my process. I wrote an algorithm that generates thousands of random brand names and have come up with hundreds of great names using it.)

So ponder the signature activity deeply. What are we absolutely incredible at? What do we love doing? Would we love doing it even if we weren't paid for it? Maybe it's doing something creative like my big ideas. Maybe it's helping people articulate their life visions or bringing harmony to their families. Maybe it's brainstorming new parts for equipment manufacturing or sourcing reliable suppliers. Maybe it's helping design a safer house for someone's elderly parents. (These are all signature activities provided by members of our program.)

When we put these three elements together, we have a value proposition that's unique, advanced, and future-proof. It also transcends the value proposition offered by our old economy competitors.

In the case of Alberta, it's stuck in the clutches of its old economy value proposition. It extracts, refines, and distributes oil and gas. That's great, I guess, as long as the price of oil is high. But what happens if it drops again? I can envision, based on Strategy No. 1: Achieve Well-Being Using Fewer Resources, that the New Economy could dramatically undermine the demand for fossil fuels. I could be wrong on that score, but it would be good for Alberta if the province had a backup plan.

I think Alberta should build its value proposition around a New Economy big idea. The province should use its oil revenues as a foundation to foster new kinds of energy: solar, wind, bio-fuels, nuclear, hydrogen, and whatever else emerges in the future. Its big goal could be to create 1,000 times more energy from non-fossil fuel sources. The province should help solve the problem of climate change and encourage anything that makes the economy more energy-efficient. But that's not what it's doing. Alberta is completely at odds with these ideas. Because it's caught in old economy thinking, it can't see the opportunities right in front of it.

I think it's folly to say we have to drop oil to save the planet. That's frankly not going to happen, at least not in the short term. But as with any other old economy business, Alberta needs a New Economy strategy, and it's in a great position to do so. I hope the province takes my advice, but I'm not sure it will. When I present these ideas, the reaction is mixed. About 50 percent agree with me; the other 50 percent don't want to hear it. Some are hostile. (That's when I pull out my Edmonton birth certificate.)

To thrive in the New Economy, build value proposition around a big idea, not a product or service. That doesn't mean abandoning a product (like oil), only that we should no longer be dependent on it. We now have more options.

STRATEGY NO. 4

Grow a Network Organically

I'VE READ SOME great business books over the past 40 years. Three of my favourites are *Positioning* by Al Ries and Jack Trout, *The Experience Economy* by B. Joseph Pine and James H. Gilmore, and *Marketing Myopia* by Theodore Levitt. These books helped me develop my business and marketing models. But the most seminal book is *What Color Is Your Parachute?* by Richard Nelson Bolles.

I read *What Color Is Your Parachute?* when I was in my late twenties. After starting and running a community newspaper called *The Uptown Magazine*, I got it in my head that I needed to get a *real* job: a nine-to-five position in an office tower downtown. I wanted a job in the marketing world, maybe at an advertising company or a public relations firm. But I wasn't sure how to get that kind of job.

Someone suggested I read *What Color Is Your Parachute?* I'm glad I did. Not only did it help me find a job, it taught me an important marketing strategy that's extremely helpful in the New Economy.

The book suggested I forgo the traditional job-seeking process where you look for employment postings and then go in for an interview. The author said this process didn't work very well because hundreds of people apply for the same job and chances are slim no matter how qualified someone is. He also said the interview process is so formal and stilted it's hard to differentiate oneself or act naturally.

So Bolles suggested another approach. He recommended building a network of contacts in a target industry. Ask people we know in an industry if we can come by their offices to learn about their businesses. Don't say we're looking for a job. Just say we want to learn. When we visit a business, ask lots of questions and discover as much as we can. Then ask if there's anyone else in the industry we can meet. Get introduced to those people and repeat the process. And one other thing: after meeting with the person, send him or her a handwritten thank-you note.

So how does this get us a job? One, it helps build a bigger network by meeting more people under less formal conditions. Two, it creates a good impression with the people we meet, especially when we send them the thank-you note. Bolles said 80 percent of jobs are never advertised. They're given to people the employer has already met.

Through this process, I visited about 50 companies and learned all about the marketing industry. Just as Bolles said, three of them offered me a job, and I accepted the best offer. It was at a public relations company with a great reputation and lots of top brand-name clients.

I only lasted two years in that job because I ultimately realized I was an entrepreneur and could never work for anyone, but the lesson of *What Color Is Your Parachute?* stayed with me. If we want to get jobs or get customers or clients, it's best to focus first on building a network. And it's better to grow this network organically, one quality person at a time.

In the New Economy, this principle is even more important. Because we live in a networked world, one of the key strategies for success is to constantly expand the size and quality of our networks. New Economy thinkers know if they start by expanding a quality network, they'll sell more. They know that a *bigger quality network equals more sales.*

While this makes total sense, old factory thinkers don't typically think that way. They focus first on selling their products and services. They expend most of their creative and intellectual energy thinking about how to sell more products. They simply head out into the marketplace and pitch their products to prospects.

In today's New Economy, the old way doesn't work very well. Robots (bots) have taken over the sales function and bombard people with computer-generated sales pitches. Faced with this flood, most prospects today block out salespeople on both the consumer level and in business-to-business situations.

To overcome this problem, follow New Economy Strategy No. 4: Grow a Network Organically. If we build a community around our businesses one quality person at a time, we'll make more sales.

Here's an example. In June 2017, I started The New Economy Network. I invited 12 of my clients to attend an event at an upscale business club. We had a spirited discussion about artificial intelligence and machine learning.

From that inaugural gathering, The New Economy Network has grown to include 300 members in five cities across North America. We've held more than 100 events. We now have sponsors, an active social media group on Mighty Networks, and an ever-expanding stable of speakers. I envision the network will continue to grow worldwide over the coming years.

I built this network slowly, one quality person at a time. I didn't just try to stack it with a bunch of people. I took my time and was very discerning. I likened the process to growing a garden. I planted the seeds by meeting lots of people, then I removed the low-quality weeds and nurtured the best plants.

Using this organic approach, I met hundreds of new people and expanded my influence. These contacts invited me to speak at dozens of events, and I got lots of new clients. And I made these sales without selling anything.

When we all worked in an assembly-line type of business, building a network wasn't necessary. We just did our specific job and went home. Our network of business relationships was very small. But in the New Economy, our success depends on the size and quality of our networks.

Think of network-building as phase one of a business or career. Give the network a name like New Economy Network. To attract people, offer something valuable for free. When people accept this free value, they become subscribers. Phase two is to turn these subscribers into customers or members. And phase three is to provide an ever-expanding value hub of products and services to members.

We can certainly buy email lists and build a large army of followers, but quality is better than quantity. Quality people in a network will spend money and help attract other high-quality people. (Note that one person's definition of high quality might be different than other people's. It doesn't just mean they have a lot of money. It means they buy into our big idea, and we enjoy working with them.)

One of my clients grew a network organically around a fashion-oriented email newsletter called *The Fashion Knowledge Network*. He started with five subscribers and now has more than five thousand. Each day he adds people from the fashion industry to his network. He focuses on quality, not quantity.

He now has a much higher profile in the fashion industry. It sees him as a leader and expert. He's been paid to give keynote speeches at conferences and has generated significant consulting revenue. He's also attracted more customers to his clothing business. He says: "By growing my network organically one person at a time, I meet more people and sell more clothing."

In the dance with robots, don't forget about people. Don't just be surrounded with technology. Reach out, build relationships.

I know for myself that I can get buried behind my screens. I can conflate social media followers with real relationships. But actually, technology can put up barriers to relationships. That's why it's still important to meet people face to face, either in person or by video conference. Ideally, in person.

It's my speculation that face-to-face meetings with real people will become precious and valuable in the New Economy. When everyone is stuck behind a screen or lost in virtual reality, encounters in the real world— what I call the bio-verse — will be treasured. An in-person meeting will be like a vinyl record compared to a streaming music service.

The bottom line is if we focus on growing a network organically, one person at a time, we'll meet more prospects and make more sales.

STRATEGY NO. 5

Ask Purpose-Driven Questions

IN THE NEW Economy, questions are more important than answers.

Andy, one of the members of my BIG Idea Adventure Program, uses this New Economy strategy to great effect. He makes a lot of money, not by having all the answers but by asking great questions. He tells his prospects: "If you meet with me, I will ask you the three most important questions you've ever been asked in your life." Of course, they want to know what the questions are. He then says: "I can't tell you; you have to come to the meeting."

At the meeting, Andy's prospects answer the three questions by thinking deeply about their lives and their businesses. At the conclusion, he tells them he has 97 other questions (100 in total), but they have to join his program, which costs $10,000 per year. To date, he's signed up more than 70 members to his multi-year program.

Andy was surprised about the success of his program. "I never thought people would pay me to ask them questions. I thought people would only pay me for answers."

In the New Economy, answers are cheap. In fact, most of the time they're free. If my wife and I have a debate about what was Brad Pitt's first movie (or another important topic), I can get the answer in two seconds on IMDb. If I want to know the weather in Pittsburgh, I can get the answer in a flash from my weather app. If I want to know the runs-batted-in for my favourite baseball player, Siri will serve up the answer while I'm brushing my teeth.

As AI becomes more powerful and the fount of data it accesses grows exponentially, robots will be the go-to source for answers about everything. Looking to a human to answer a question on a specific topic will seem odd and a waste of time.

This reality will hit people hard who think their storehouses of knowledge are their most important assets. No matter how much knowledge people have stored in their brains, it will never match the storehouse of knowledge resident in the global AI data bank. That's why it's important to shift the human focus to skillful questioning.

Case in point. In an act of male overconfidence, according to my astute wife, I decided to re-grout some of the logs in our cabin. The trick is to properly mix the plaster in the exact proportions so it isn't too watery or too dry. You also have to apply the plaster within a very specific time frame. Once mixed, the plaster must be used within 20 minutes. Tricky.

To undertake this task, I consulted with the guys at the local building supply store. They explained how to mix the three ingredients: sand, cement, and lime. They gave me a specific ratio for the three elements. So far, so good. But when I mixed it, it didn't work. The mix was too watery and didn't adhere to the space between the logs. I was confused because I had done exactly what the guys at the building centre had told me to do.

That's when I turned to the internet. I asked Google questions about my problem. Why is the plaster mix too watery? If I'm using ABC-brand cement, does that change the lime ratio in the mix? What happens if you combine ABC-brand cement with XYZ-brand lime? Does that change anything? Sure enough, Google directed me to the very specific information I needed. It turned out that I had to double the amount of lime in the mixture, which I did promptly. That made the plaster just the right consistency.

At the time, I was amazed I could get such specific answers from the internet. If it had been 20 years earlier, I would have been completely at a loss. But then I realized that I had played a vital part in the dance. I had asked the right questions of the robot. Without my adroit multi-layered inquiry, I wouldn't have ascertained the right answer.

Just a final note on the whole affair. A minute before I was to apply the plaster mixture, we had a power failure. All the lights went out. So I had to quickly rig a battery-powered lighting system to do the job before the plaster set. It was absolutely crazy, but the final result was quite good.

Learning how to ask great questions and then build on those questions is a key skill in the New Economy. We ask questions of both humans and robots. We get good at listening to the answers and then ask further questions.

Even more important, we start by defining our purpose. We ask ourselves: What do we really want to accomplish? What is our underlying motivation and intention? Why do we want to accomplish this outcome?

With a clear purpose in mind, we come up with better questions to ask the robots. As in the case with my plaster job, I had a specific outcome in mind. I kept asking detailed questions until the robot gave me the answer I needed.

So replace storehousing with purpose-seeking. Replace answering with questioning. And don't just ask about what, ask about who. Who can help accomplish our purpose? Does the robot know someone who can help us? Ask the robot to help build new connections with both humans and robots.

In this dance with robots, we use our Human Superpower of unbridled curiosity. We take the fetters off. We roam far and wide with our curiosity. We never stop asking questions.

When we take this path, we discover that purpose-driven questions open infinite possibilities. In school, I always sat in the first row (I was a total browner) and kept asking questions. I could never understand the kids who sat at the back and never asked a question. I was simply curious about everything. And I liked asking questions because the answers opened up new worlds for me. Each answer led to another bunch of questions. There was no end to the possible questions I could ask. I guess that's why I became a writer and a journalist; I had so many questions.

So get curious. Start with a purpose. Never stop asking questions. We never know where our questions will take us.

STRATEGY NO. 6

Transcend and Integrate

AS THEY CIRCLED the moon on Christmas Eve 1968, the astronauts aboard Apollo 8 — Frank Borman, James Lovell, and William Anders — broadcast a televised greeting to the world. The Apollo 8 crew were the first humans to orbit the moon. They didn't land on the lunar surface — that was Apollo 11 — but they proved that a lunar orbit was feasible.

I was 11 years old. In the darkness driving home from a Christmas party, I listened awestruck to their message broadcast on our car radio. They read passages from the Book of Genesis. It was a powerful, transcendent moment for humanity.

The astronauts also took a stunning photograph that night, a picture of our blue planet set against the deep black background of space. In this image of Earth, there are no countries, no borders, no races, no political parties. Just a tiny planet floating in space.

On Earth, in our businesses and lives, we think we live in a world of boundaries and borders, of categories and subcategories, definitions and further definitions. But they're not real. They're ideas we collectively construct in our minds. These "social constructs" are useful because they help us make sense of our experiences, but they also keep us trapped in narrow definitions and limit our potential. We build a prison in our minds to keep us safe and then become both the prisoner and the warden.

Social constructs also fragment our thinking. When we create categories for everything, we separate everything. We no longer see the whole, we see parts, and we lose sight of how these parts fit together. We then become attached to our parts and cling to them desperately.

For this reason, old factory thinkers and their organizations tend to be fragmented and self-limited. They say: We make spoons, but not forks. We teach math, but not history. We sell running shoes, not swimsuits. They adhere to a narrowly defined value proposition and paint themselves into a corner. And strangely, no one's telling them to do it. They just think that's what they should do.

Dividing, categorizing, and comparing makes us hyper-competitive. We define ourselves, stake out our category, and strive to become the best player in that category. We abhor our rivals and want to crush them.

The problem is, we can never win this game. As I learned from playing tennis, there's always a better player. (See my book *Going to the Net* about the psychology of tennis.) No matter how hard we strive, someone will inevitably top us. Even if we reign at the top of our category for decades, we'll always feel the sharks nipping at our heels, and one day they'll devour us. It's not a great way to live or run a business. But most of us think it's the only game in town.

Furthermore, fragmented thinking stops us from seeing the more transcendent integrated value we could provide to our customers. When we fight it out to win the war for dominance of our category, we don't see that our customers would actually benefit by having all the categories brought together and unified in the service of a higher value.

The key is to give up the war, give up the competition, transcend and integrate.

Let me give an example. Let's say someone owns a flower shop that's number one in its marketplace. That sounds good, but it's a booby prize. Nothing is actually won. With lots of competition, the proprietor can't raise prices for fear of losing market share and a dominant position. No matter what's done, sooner or later a competitor will usurp the top position.

In the New Economy, it's easy for customers to see all the competitors in an industry or product category. They can then quickly compare and choose the best option at the lowest price. (I wrote a book about this issue called *The Problem with Penguins*.)

That's why in the New Economy, we can't win this competition, so don't try. Instead, assume a more transcendent position. Flower shop owners should create a platform that integrates all flower shops and launch a portal that gives customers a single access point to every flower shop, including the most bitter rivals. Turn competitors into strategic partners. Charge them a fee to be part of the network. In other words, make money from competitors.

Then take it further: integrate. Add value components that complement flowers. Add event planners, catering, gift baskets, greeting cards, entertainers like balladeers, romantic experiences, and chocolate. Curate and integrate top-quality suppliers and monetize them.

This sounds simple and it is, as long as we have the right mindset. If we're caught up in competition, we'll never transcend and integrate. We'll never co-operate with our competitors.

The fact that most of our competitors will never transcend and integrate is a competitive advantage. By adopting a transcendent mindset, we set up a very strong barrier to entry. To enter our transcendent space, our competitors also have to adopt a transcendent mindset, which is very hard to do if they're caught in old economy thinking.

Transcendence is also about appreciating the potential of a higher-level value proposition. In the case of our enlightened flower shop, the proprietor realizes that customers aren't just flower lovers; they're lovers. They don't just buy flowers because they love roses; they buy flowers because they love Rose or Ronald. Instead of being in the flower business, our proprietor realizes he or she is in the romance business. (I know this first-hand because I won over my wife, Ginny, by sending her a dazzling bouquet of flowers after our second date.)

By adopting a transcendent value proposition (romance, not flowers), we lose interest in competing. We see that winning the flower fight is a bantamweight battle. Sweet revenge, if that's what we want, is to make money whenever someone buys our competitor's flowers. Wouldn't that be amazing? It's also fun to make passive income by selling products and services that aren't in our normal industry or category.

My business soared after I decided to transcend and integrate. For the first 10 years, we sold marketing services like newsletter publishing, graphic design, and website development. But competition was fierce, and our profit margins were anemic.

After some reflection, I concluded we were like marketing plumbers. We provided marketing pipes. So we decided to become marketing architects — to help our clients create marketing blueprints and then bring together all the marketing products and services they needed, whether we produced them or not. Our BIG Idea Adventure Program was born.

Transcending and integrating was a good move for our company because it provided a higher level of value to our clients. They needed a marketing architect more than they needed a marketing plumber. They could get a marketing plumber anywhere. But marketing architects were much rarer. In fact, since we started our program in 1998, we have yet to see any of our competitors make a similar transcendent shift. We have, however, integrated a number of them into our value hub.

Transcendence and integration, of course, includes robots. When we take the high road, we stop competing with robots and see them instead as useful suppliers and partners. Although we think of technology as natural integrators (think integrated circuits and software compilers), they're actually not that great at integrating. Most technology is very specific in its functions. For example, a voice-to-text app is good at voice to text, but not so good at taking blood pressure. Or a system that analyzes the DNA structure of a virus isn't very good at analyzing the buying habits of teenagers.

Technology is also not great at transcending. Even the most robust machine learning algorithm is going to stay in its lane no matter how smart it gets. If the AI is set up to automate and optimize the logistics of a grocery-delivery company, it's not suddenly going to propose new nutrition standards or bring together all the grocery chains into a co-operative online platform.

So we humans have a huge competitive advantage when it comes to transcendent value creation. We're masters at it. By using embodied pattern recognition and our propensity for purpose-driven ideation, we discern higher-level problems in the world and come up with new ideas to provide a higher level of value. We also see how previously disparate concepts, resources, and technology can be integrated for more meaningful and beneficent purposes.

Ask: So what does transcendence mean for us? What is our higher-level value proposition? What higher-level role can we assume? How can we integrate disparate resources on behalf of our customers? How can we co-operate with our competitors?

STRATEGY NO. 7

Dematerialize

FOR MANY YEARS, I harboured an unquenchable passion for Perrier, the French mineral water. I constantly craved a cold Perrier with a slice of lime. Like many things in my life, my passion was a tad overboard. I drank two or three large bottles a day, which meant I had to buy at least three cases every week from the grocery store. Of course, Perrier loved me. I reckoned I was in its top 1 percent of customers. But I wasn't going to win any environmental awards. Perrier had to extract the water, put it in bottles created from raw materials, and then ship the cases across the Atlantic Ocean to my local store. Then I went to the store in my car, lugged the cases into my house, and then, after I consumed the product, the bottles had to be recycled. That's pretty crazy when you think about it. My Perrier passion took a mammoth amount of time, effort, and energy, not to mention cash.

Then SodaStream came along. Talk about disruption. Now we make our bubbly water at home. And while I still like the taste of Perrier, the money, time, and energy we save using SodaStream is hard to ignore. So now I rarely buy Perrier (sorry, Perrier); I use SodaStream. And yes, it's true I have to replace the gas canisters regularly, but SodaStream is much better for the environment. I no longer lug cases of Perrier to my house and no longer fill up the recycling bin with used bottles. I also save money.

SodaStream is an example of "dematerialization" — a new technology or way of doing things that requires fewer resources and delivers a similar, if not superior, result. More specifically, the value received requires fewer resources, especially tangible resources extracted from the earth. Dematerialization is a powerful trend in the New Economy that few people understand and recognize.

In his book *More for Less*, author Andrew McAfee explains that economic growth is no longer tied to the increased extraction of resources from the planet. In fact, during the past 30 years, economic growth has gone up while resource extraction has gone down. McAfee stresses that this trend is unprecedented. Over the previous 1,000 years, all economic growth was tied directly to the increased extraction of resources. But in the 1990s, companies began to employ computers to figure out how to get better results using fewer resources or inputs.

For example, a can of Coca-Cola today utilizes one-tenth the aluminum used 30 years ago. We still get the tasty cola, but the transport mechanism, the can, weighs much less. And here's the key point. Consumers don't care about the weight of the can. We don't buy the can; we buy the drink. So Coca-Cola can use less aluminum and lower its costs without losing market share. That's a powerful incentive. Like Coca-Cola, every producer wants to lower its costs. That increases profit. That's why every company has an inherent imperative in the New Economy to dematerialize.

In the coming years, the fact of dematerialization will become more apparent. Everything will get lighter and leaner, and many things will simply disappear. Think about the smartphone. We no longer need a camera, calculator, scanner, notepad, stereo system, television, fax machine, mailing machine, or even computer. They've all been replaced by smartphones, which have also replaced DVDs and DVD players; printed books, newspapers, and catalogues; and a host of medical equipment. Even bookshelves. Why do we need them if all our books and DVDs have been dematerialized?

Dematerialization means all metals, fossil fuels, water, and wood that were formerly required to manufacture, distribute, store, and sell these products are no longer necessary. They can stay in the earth.

The news about dematerialization terrifies anyone who works in the resource-extraction industry. If we make money pulling things from the earth, we don't want to hear about dematerialization. But it should also set off alarms for anyone who makes money from anything tangible.

Now don't get me wrong. We'll still need tangible things like cars, clothes, and houses, but these items will be produced using fewer tangible resources. That's because manufacturers using increasingly faster computers and more powerful engineering software will be motivated to lower their costs by employing fewer resources. And here's another key point. It's not because these companies want to save the planet, they'll dematerialize their products and inputs because they want to save money.

Money is a great example of dematerialization. I used to carry around a bulky wad of paper money and coins. But now I rarely carry any money in my pocket. I do my retail transactions with a tap of my Apple Watch. (Oops, there goes the wallet and credit cards.) And as a merchant, I no longer have a credit-card machine. We use an online system for our business.

More dramatically, 10 years ago I had an office with dozens of people working in it. That required a plethora of desks, chairs, and computers, along with a kitchen, a water cooler, and tons of other pieces of equipment. That was my old factory.

Let's say the combined weight of that equipment was 10 tonnes. That's a lot of stuff extracted from the earth. It also cost me a bundle to buy and maintain. Today, my business weighs about 1 tonne, yet we provide even more value to our customers.

The dematerialization of my business wasn't something that just happened; I did it deliberately. A decade ago, I set the goal to get rid of as much stuff as possible while doubling the value we deliver to our clients. I appreciated that my clients didn't give a hoot about our 10-tonne pile of stuff; they just wanted to get value from us. I also realized that making my business lighter meant I could spend less time managing my stuff and more time helping our clients.

Dematerialization is happening imperceptibly. Every day we extract fewer resources from the earth and get higher economic returns. Let that sink in because that's not the way most people see it. Most folks assume we're depleting the earth as the economy grows, and therefore the only way to save the planet is to cut back on economic growth. That's the epitome of old economy thinking because that notion might have been true 40 years ago, but it's not true today.

Also, dematerialization is made possible because of the competitive nature and profit motive inherent in the capitalist system. Nowadays, it's trendy to say that capitalism is evil, but capitalism actually drives dematerialization. Left to their own devices and subject to competitive market forces, producers have an incentive to use fewer resource inputs in order to lower their costs and increase their profits. Consumers also have an incentive to buy products and services that save them time, money, and effort and utilize fewer tangible resources.

Paradoxically, I also believe in regulation as long it's done for the right reasons. Regulating that cars should be more fuel-efficient is good for car manufacturers because it encourages them to lower their input costs and also makes their cars more attractive to consumers. A fine balance between capitalism and regulation works best in the New Economy.

Ten years from now everything will be significantly lighter. Many things will disappear, yet we'll have greater prosperity. We'll look back and realize that we moved beyond products and services into a world of intangible value (see my book *Beyond Basketballs*).

The implications of this New Economy strategy are profound. Once we get our heads around the facts of dematerialization, we naturally start to get rid of stuff. As I did, we might get rid of our big offices. (The Covid-19 pandemic accelerated this trend.) By dematerializing our operations, we'll save time, money, and effort and be able to create and provide more value to our customers.

I ask my clients how much time they spend providing value to customers. They often say 10 to 20 percent at best. Then I ask them what they're doing with the rest of their time. They're often not sure. But I know. They spend 80 to 90 percent of their time looking after their stuff. Their old economy thinking makes them believe their stuff is their business.

That's why the road forward is to get rid of as much stuff as possible (for example, 10 tonnes down to 225 kilograms or less). We'll then have 80 to 90 percent of our time and energy available to help our customers.

Moreover, we can devote more of our time to help our customers dematerialize. We can ponder these questions:

1. How can we help our customers get better results using fewer resources?
2. What intangible value can we create that replaces something tangible?
3. How can we use New Economy technology to develop dematerialized value?
4. What would our businesses (our new factories) look like if they were completely virtual?

One last point for clarification. Not everything in the New Economy will disappear. That's not the objective. The mandate is to get rid of anything tangible that isn't necessary or desirable. We might still want to buy vinyl records because we like the feel and sound of them. (Sales of vinyl records boomed during the pandemic.) But the trend line is clear: most things will dematerialize and become either smaller or lighter or vanish altogether.

STRATEGY NO. 8

Mass-Customize

IN THE OLD economy, we could pump out the same product or service over and over again. When I worked in the brewery, we bottled the same beer for two years. When I did my stint on the hot dog stand, we sold the same hot dogs. I won't even mention the two weeks I spent making candy floss. *Yuk!*

The old economy was all about mass production. Henry Ford perfected the assembly line for cars and then everyone tried to apply the same principle in their businesses. Everything was mass-produced: hamburgers, insurance policies, and hats. As Henry Ford quipped: "You can have your automobile in any colour you want as long as it's black."

But in our dance with robots, mass production doesn't work anymore. In the New Economy, we must quickly respond to our customers' ever-shifting desires and provide them with a unique package of value. They want a custom-designed hamburger or hot dog. They want a personalized insurance policy. They want to wear a one-of-a-kind hat.

To succeed in the New Economy, our businesses must be designed to provide mass-customization, which means being able to provide a customized result for each customer, but also do it expeditiously and profitably.

In my book *The Strategic Enterprise*, I articulated the key entrepreneurial benefit of mass-customization. It helps us to quickly seize profitable and unforeseen opportunities as they arise. In the New Economy, the fleet of foot win the day. Our customers won't wait around for us to give them what they want. They're impatient. If we hesitate and can't pull together a unique solution quickly, our customers will seek a supplier that can.

I wrote *The Strategic Enterprise* in 2000. Mass-customization was important then, but it's even more essential now. The rise of robots and other pervasive technology is accelerating change in the economy. What worked last week might not work today. What worked an hour ago might not work now. In order to stay relevant, businesses must be continually responsive to here and now. In our dance with robots, there's no past, no future. There's just here and now.

So mass-customization is a good idea, but how do we pull it off? What does a mass-customization system look like? How do we build one? Fortunately, I discovered a universal mass-customization process. It is, in fact, a mass-customization system for creating a mass-customization system. (Take a moment to process that mind-bender!)

This universal mass-customization process is quite simple, yet very powerful. It will help us prosper in the New Economy and future-proof our businesses. It's also universal, in the sense that it can be applied to any kind of business.

Before I explain this universal mass-customization process, let's pause for a short overview. In the old economy, the assembly line was the foundational means of production. As I said, virtually every old economy business was designed as an assembly line.

Assembly lines are a linear process. We take raw material as an input, produce a finished good or service, and then distribute it to the marketplace. This process is straightforward but fraught with vulnerabilities. What if we produce the wrong product? What if the market changes? How can we change a process that produces kitty litter to one that creates dog collars? It's not so easy. That's why so many factories closed in the Rust Belt. Those old plants and their assembly lines were designed to produce specific products and were summarily abandoned when the products they produced were no longer marketable.

However, if we build a new factory around a mass-customization process, we'll never have to abandon it. It will constantly churn out what people want and need because it's specifically designed for a constantly changing marketplace and is structured to meet the unique needs of each customer. It can produce kitty litter for one customer and a dog collar for the one after that, or even accessories for a pet robot!

The key distinction between the typical old economy business process and the New Economy business process is intention. With the old economy process, the intention is to furnish a customer with a specific predetermined product or service. The role of the salesperson is to sell the prospect a specific product.

With the New Economy process, the intention is to first investigate what's really required, then provide whatever the customer actually wants. The role of the salesperson is to determine what the customer really needs and respond accordingly. So if we think the customer desires a hammer, but we find out they really want or need a screwdriver, we're willing and able to pivot to screwdrivers.

Interestingly, even customers might not know at the start of the process what they really need. They might think they need a hammer. But through this process, they discover, too, that they actually need a screwdriver. This process is an act of open-minded collaboration between the buyer and seller.

So let's take a look at this universal mass-customization process. It has nine stages:

Stage 1: Assess the Current Situation — When prospects or customers are met, start by assessing their current situations. What's working and what isn't? How do they feel about their current states? Are they feeling happy and confident or worried and frustrated? Don't try to solve their problems at this stage, just use the Human Superpower of unbridled curiosity. Ask great questions and listen deeply.

Stage 2: Create a Vision — Help customers or clients craft a vision for their futures. What are their long-range goals? What do they really want to achieve? Encourage them to think big. Use the Human Superpower of purpose-driven ideation to suggest potential ideas to include in their visions and have them write them down.

Stage 3: Identify Roadblocks — What are the factors that might stop them from the achievement of their visions? Is there a lack of resources? Are they stymied by mental blocks? Will they get resistance from other people or institutions? While this stage might sound negative, it's part of Strategy No. 10: Embrace Radical Reality, which is explained in an upcoming chapter.

Stage 4: Develop Strategies to Overcome Roadblocks — For each delineated roadblock, brainstorm strategies and tactics to deal with them. Drill down to create micro-strategies for even the smallest micro-roadblocks. Bring purpose-driven ideation into service during this stage.

Stage 5: Select Resources — Identify what resources customers need. These resources will include products and services but could also involve external resources provided by other organizations. This is where the concept of the value hub comes in. Be ready to integrate all the required resources for customers and reap the first major financial payoff of the universal process.

Stage 6: Build a Team — At this stage, help customers pull together a consortium of experts, suppliers, and supporters. This team of people and robots will have a unique configuration for each customer and for each situation.

Stage 7: Implement a Plan — During this stage, coordinate the implementation of the strategies, the accessing of resources, and the coordination of the team, acting as the general contractor.

Stage 8: Review Progress Regularly — It's critical to reconvene with customers periodically to assess progress. What have they accomplished so far? Why is this accomplishment important? How can we build on this progress? Celebrate even the smallest accomplishment to keep customers motivated and determined to stay on track.

Stage 9: Review and Refine the Plan Regularly — This stage takes the process back to the beginning. Review customers' current situations. Update their visions. Identify new roadblocks and develop new strategies. Select new resources and realign the team. Continue to implement. (Note: This is the key step in the process. It ensures that relationships with customers don't devolve into a rigid structure on a single track that provides a static set of value components.)

That's the universal mass-customization process. It can be used in any situation and in any industry. I've taught hundreds of companies to employ it, such as funeral homes, health-care providers, manufacturers, yogurt stores, insurance companies, and airlines.

The universal mass-customization process can be delivered in a myriad of ways. It can be facilitated in person, remotely, or in an automated fashion. It can be done quickly or over an extended period of time. Customers can be coached through it or they can do it themselves.

Universal mass-customization is an important New Economy strategy because it helps bring order to a constantly changing world that's also increasingly complex. Instead of simply selecting or putting forth a singular resource or technology, we judiciously discern the best possible course of action for each unique situation. And most importantly, we help our customers achieve the visions they really want.

STRATEGY NO. 9

Facilitate Flow

THE BIBLE STORY I remember most from Sunday School is the tale of the seven fat cows and the seven skinny cows. In the story, Joseph is sold into Egypt as a slave and becomes an adviser to the Pharoah. One night, the Pharoah has a dream about seven fat cows followed by seven thin cows. Joseph says the dream foretells that Egypt will experience seven years of plenty followed by seven years of famine. Based on this interpretation, the Pharoah takes measures to store food and grain during the time of abundance, thereby saving Egypt from starvation during the famine.

It's a good story. I thought it was cool how Joseph becomes popular with the Pharoah because of his talent for dream analysis. But it's the economic lesson of the story that stuck with me most. (I was even thinking about economics in church at eight years of age!) The lesson is: When we make hay while the sun shines, be sure to save some of it for rainy days. Make sure to storehouse some of our harvest to tide us over for the lean times.

That's great advice that I've used all my life (glad my mom was a Sunday school teacher!). But in the New Economy, this parable is obsolete because storehousing is no longer a winning strategy. Instead of storehousing, it's better and more profitable to facilitate flow. Instead of being a storekeeper, be a flow facilitator.

For example, when I attended university, my objective was to gather up a storehouse of knowledge about a range of subjects with one major topic at the core of my academic endeavours (economics). The strategy was to take that storehouse out in the marketplace and build a career around what I had learned.

As you might know from reading my other books, my career path wasn't a straight traditional trajectory. After pursuing a liberal arts degree, I acquired a bachelor of arts in journalism and learned how to write. But the most important knowledge I accumulated in those days was working as a waiter (see my book *How to Sell a Lobster*). But all along, the notion was that the way to achieve success was to accumulate and store knowledge and then to peddle that knowledge in the marketplace.

The compulsion to accumulate and storehouse is deeply ingrained in our collective psyche. The more stuff we gather up, the more prosperous and secure we feel. But we also become very protective of our stash and spend a lot of resources to defend it. This storehousing can lead to inequality, injustice, and even war. If we think about it, most wars have been fought between one group of people trying to get the other group's stash of stuff. To the winner, go the spoils.

The questionable upside of storehousing has now been permanently upended in the New Economy. In a world that changes relentlessly in an unpredictable fashion, whatever we storehouse might not be ultimately marketable. For example, let's take an expert in Lotus 1-2-3 in the 1990s. It was IBM's most popular killer application at the time. Such experts had more knowledge stored up about Lotus 1-2-3 than anyone in the world. But in 2013, Lotus 1-2-3 was discontinued, and suddenly, the accumulated storehouse was useless. Storing up seven fat cows of knowledge about Lotus 1-2-3 did no good once the marketplace changed.

Of course, things change even faster these days. Any golden nugget of knowledge stored up today might be fool's gold tomorrow. This problem applies equally to any kind of tangible product or equipment. Any physical thing we storehouse could be useless or woefully outdated in very short order. That's why most department stores have been eviscerated by the New Economy. Their entire purpose was to act as a "store" house where shoppers could find what they wanted. But it was the cost of storing things and the embedded lack of flexibility in that business model that have doomed department stores in the age of Amazon and online shopping.

For these reasons, the better approach in the New Economy is to facilitate flow, to set ourselves up as the conduit of value between two or more parties, figure out how to make it easy for a value creator to provide that value to a value consumer. We don't need to create our own value packages; we simply facilitate flow, which is a much higher level of value in itself.

As I mentioned earlier, I created The New Economy Network, which has grown from a small cadre of business owners in Toronto to an ever-expanding community that spans the world. My vision was to facilitate the flow of knowledge and resources from New Economy experts to business owners who need help to navigate the realities of this new marketplace.

I've brought in speakers to talk about artificial intelligence, the blockchain, and the IoT. My objective isn't to impart my storehouse of knowledge on the subject but to facilitate the flow of the infinitely larger fount of other people's constantly expanding knowledge. Interestingly, by being the flow facilitator who curates this information value hub, my knowledge has grown much bigger than would have been possible previously, and my status as a New Economy expert has been enhanced.

One of my clients had tremendous success as a flow facilitator. He created a network platform for the firefighting industry. His popular platform consisted of an email newsletter he sent out twice a month. The publication featured links to YouTube videos and other internet content about trends in the firefighting industry. It took about 20 minutes to pull together each issue. He didn't produce any content of his own. The results were spectacular. He had hundreds of firefighters in his network. They loved his curated content. My client was invited to give keynote speeches at industry events and sold more firefighting equipment, all because he acted as a flow facilitator.

A mental switch is needed to fully embrace the difference between storehousing and flow. In storehousing mode, we might conduct a lot of research to enhance our knowledge about a certain topic. We might use this knowledge to provide a product or service to customers. We might write a blog or a book. Ideally, we would recycle this same knowledge over and over again.

In flow mode, we don't storehouse knowledge. We discover great knowledge and resources and pass it on to other people in our networks. Time is of the essence. We know that knowledge and resources have a short lifespan in the New Economy so we don't hang on to anything; we pass it on. We can earn money directly by charging people for access to our flows. We can use our flows as a marketing tool to attract prospects to our traditional products and services. Or we can earn commissions from value creators when our customers buy their value packages on our platforms.

Bloggers or content creators might want to change their approaches. Think of the time and effort spent creating content. Is it worth the effort? Perhaps we would gain more influence being content conduits rather than content creators. In my case, I chose to take the middle way. I still create some content (like this book) because I love the creation process. But I also act as a flow facilitator.

Facilitating flow is a new value set. It's transcendent value because it solves key problems inherent in the New Economy. One problem is information overload. By serving as discerning curators, we make it easier for our audiences to get high-quality content that's been carefully selected. We've done the searching and vetting for them. Second, it solves the lifespan problem. We put fresh, timely information into their hands. And third, it solves our problem, which I call "feeding the beast." If we're content creators, we have to keep feeding the beast, constantly writing blogs and producing videos. As a flow facilitator, we leverage the efforts of others and in exchange give them some exposure.

In my book *Strategic Marketing for the Digital Age*, I introduced an analogy for flow facilitation. At the time, the concept was light years ahead of the curve for most people. I said that it was better to own a train station than the railway. Running a railway is risky. Trains have to be kept filled with passengers, not to mention all the maintenance on them. I said it was better to own the train station that serves as the nexus of the traffic: people, trains, subways, buses, and cars. The job is to be the grand central station and facilitate the flow of traffic. Let other people run the railway. Stop storehousing. Facilitate flow.

STRATEGY NO. 10

Embrace Radical Reality

WHEN I WAS 15 years old, I read *1984,* the dystopian novel by George Orwell. In Orwell's world, Big Brother keeps a constant eye on citizens, using surveillance cameras inside their homes. Employing doublespeak and other forms of brainwashing (today, called gaslighting), the overlords convince people to believe anything even if it contradicts what they were led to believe the day before. In fact, the point of doublespeak is to render people incapable of discerning truth from fiction until they don't even bother to try anymore. As in all prophetic novels, such as *Brave New World* and *The Handmaid's Tale,* the authors' purpose is to help us avoid such a fate, discern the early-warning signs of dictatorship and fascism, and snuff them out in their embryonic stage.

Books like *1984* give us a glimpse of a possible future, but of course the future never turns out exactly the way we predict. It takes twists and turns we couldn't imagine. Orwell thought Big Brother would brainwash us, but that's not how it's turned out. In the New Economy, we brainwash ourselves with the help of algorithms. We brainwash ourselves by creating our own alternative reality, by forming around us a digital bubble of news sources, influencers, and fellow travellers who share our own version of the "truth." This personally constructed reality brainwashes us to believe the most outlandish conspiracy theories such as Pizzagate (Hillary Clinton runs a child sex-trafficking ring under a pizza shop), or the pantheon of villains that populate QAnon conspiracy theories (for instance, a global deep-state cabal that drinks the blood of children to stay forever young). And then there's the rise of boutique extremist groups such as incels (young men bent on seeking revenge on women), the Proud Boys, and ISIS. All of these congregations and their attendant belief systems are made possible by the internet and social media, which enable disparate groups of people to come together around a common idea or narrative, even the most ridiculous or far-fetched. I call these common ideas or narratives belief bubbles.

While the rise of extremist groups and conspiracy theories on the internet is a well-known phenomenon, what interests me is the fact that these cult-like structures often don't have single leaders who started them and built followings. Typically, a belief bubble originates with a single cell of information that begins to attract the attention of a small number of people. This small info-organism grows with the introduction of new ancillary ideas, concepts, or opinions that latch on to it. Quickly, the belief bubble reaches the hyper-growth stage as a crowd (or mob) gravitates around the core ideas of the conspiracy or movement. This process can occur over a few hours or days without any single person or group necessarily orchestrating it. However, that being said, it's common for opportunists or provocateurs to rush in to exploit the rise of new belief bubbles.

When a belief bubble reaches its full maturity, it can have millions of adherents who have developed a sense of self and community around its core tenants. It makes them feel powerful and connected. It also leads them to seek out further information that reinforces their belief and to try to draw more people into the bubble in order to validate their beliefs. After a while, it's no longer about the content of the conspiracy theory; it's about who they are as persons. That's why it's hard to convince such people that their conspiracy theories are wrong and that they've been brainwashed. Because they actually brainwashed themselves, it's hard to deprogram them. Their versions of reality are completely different from ours, and that's one of the biggest issues in the New Economy. What do we do as a society when we don't all share the same basic building blocks of truth, when everyone can build their own bespoke versions of reality?

That's the reason Strategy No. 10 is Embrace Radical Reality. We need to take a radical approach to how we construct our sense of reality from the ground up. Otherwise, we might get swept away by a belief bubble that doesn't have our best interests at heart.

When I decided to pursue journalism, I was idealistic. In the interview for journalism school, I told the professor I wanted to write stories so people would understand what was true and what wasn't. I believed, and still do, that journalism is a noble profession and a key element of democracy. The professor liked the sound of my convictions and accepted my application.

But when I dug deeper into journalism, I discovered that it could be used not only for good but also for bad. I read about William Randolph Hearst and Henry Luce, two powerful American publishers who utilized journalism to manipulate public opinion and promote their versions of reality. Hearst, for example, engaged in an ongoing vendetta with the San Francisco transit authority to rile up his readers and boost circulation. In one case, he paid someone to jump off a public transit ferry so he could run a front-page story about the "fact" that the transit authority didn't care about the safety of its ferry passengers. Call it manufactured outrage.

Henry Luce, the founding publisher of *Time*, employed his power to promote far-right political beliefs, primarily by using China and Mao Zedong as punching bags. Many of the stories Luce published were stuffed with half-truths, quarter-truths, or total fabrications. Luce created a belief bubble long before the internet.

These two classic examples of reality-making raised my awareness of media manipulation. I could see that most media outlets, from small-town newspapers to megalithic media companies, have an underlying political agenda and belief system they foist upon their constituencies. This isn't necessarily good or bad. The objectives of publishers and journalism might be well intentioned, but it can't be denied that their general narratives reflect certain beliefs and their versions of reality. This heightened awareness was ultimately the most useful outcome of my journalism training because it protected me from being brainwashed by the media. I was now better equipped to consume the content of the media while also being better able to recognize the underlying reality-making agenda of media providers. (But don't get me wrong. I just got better at it. I didn't get perfect at it. In many cases, I'm sure I've been brainwashed by the media because the number one feature of being brainwashed is that you don't know you're brainwashed!)

So why am I relating all this? Because it's important to realize that belief manipulation, belief bubbles, and all their attendant repercussions aren't new phenomena. It's been going on since before recorded time, but like many things, this issue has become bigger and more dangerous in the New Economy. It's also become different in how it manifests and how we can manage it. We must develop our capacity to maintain a valid and helpful grasp on reality, to discern what's real and what isn't. We must take a radical approach.

Consider deepfake videos. It's now quite easy to produce fake videos that show someone saying and doing things that never happened. There's a deepfake video of Richard Nixon speaking from the Oval Office announcing the deaths of the Apollo 11 astronauts who perished on the moon. Of course, that's not what happened, but the video is totally convincing. The computer-generated character in the video looks like Nixon, talks like Nixon, and if we didn't know better, we'd be convinced it is Nixon, We could be persuaded that he actually said those things. We could also believe that Neil Armstrong and Buzz Aldrin died on the moon.

Imagine if someone malicious decided to make a deepfake video of a U.S. president announcing the launch of a salvo of nuclear missiles at Russia or China. Suddenly, it appears on our Facebook or Twitter feeds. It looks real. Is it real? How would we react? More importantly, how would Russia or China react? With only minutes to discern the veracity of the video, would Russia or China be compelled to launch a counterattack just in case?

What happens if a deepfake video emerges on election day showing a candidate engaged in a heinous crime or some debauchery? It looks real? Is it real? Could it affect the vote?

What if someone produces a deepfake video of us? What if our social media history is scoured by nefarious actors who collect our selfies? What if the resulting deepfake video is posted on the internet and shared with millions of people? How could we prove this wasn't really us? Even if we did convince the world that it isn't us, the salacious stain of it might be impossible to rub off. (This has happened to many women who have been victimized by their former partners using a deeply damaging form of deepfake video: deepfake revenge porn.)

We're entering a future where it will be increasingly difficult to discern what's true from what isn't. Our reality will be shaped more and more by what we experience in the digital world where a lot of what we consume will be fake. If we're not careful, we could find ourselves deeply entrenched in a malevolent belief bubble. (And remember, the key feature of a belief bubble is that we don't think we're in a belief bubble.)

So embrace radical reality. Become a belief-bubble anarchist and burst bubbles. Start with the notion that all of us are in a belief bubble. It might not be a QAnon or Pizzagate bubble. It might be populated by teddy bears and cookie recipes, but it's indeed a bubble. Look at it. Describe the bubble. Appreciate why we've embraced a bubble in the first place. Does it make us feel safe? Does it make us feel connected? Does it stir up strong emotions? Does it get us angry? Is it helping us and the world?

Then identify the structure of the bubble. Who are we connected to? Who have we blocked? What media are we using? What are their inherent belief systems? What are they for and against? Are they credible? Are they well-meaning? What's in it for them? Are they trying to help us or manipulate us?

In his book *Becoming Human*, Jean Vanier discusses the role of tribalism and group dynamics as an integral element of the human experience. Vanier encourages us to form groups, associations, and communities with great care and self-awareness. He points to one form of community that's defined by who and what it excludes, and another form of community that defines itself based on common goals and beliefs but doesn't make exclusion and identity the core of its reason for being. Vanier encourages communities that are designed to connect with and embrace other communities — a network of networks!

Becoming human and staying human will be core practices in the dance with robots. Being human means honouring that we all have more in common as human beings rather than what's different about us (see Strategy No. 29: Be Human). This perspective can help us recognize the contours and strictures of our personal belief bubbles. We can see if we're working on an exclusion project (blocking and trolling), or if we're working on an inclusion project (connecting and empowering).

By embracing radical reality, we also construct our own clear-eyed sense of reality by understanding that reality is, in fact, constructed. For instance, what colour is grass? Green? But is grass actually green? What looks like green is actually the green light waves being reflected by the grass and then interpreted in our minds as green. In truth, grass isn't green. We constructed green in our minds. The reality "green" is just a convenient invention. We don't actually know what the world really looks like. What does grass look like? We don't know. We can only invent our versions of it.

What's true about grass and green is true about everything. What is a car? It's a vehicle that takes us from A to B. But what makes up a car? Are the tires the car? Is the steering wheel the car? Is the engine the car? No. A car is an aggregate of these parts. There's nothing to point to that describes the inherent essence of the car. Like everything else, a car is actually a concept we've constructed in our minds.

So like it or not, we construct reality in our minds. It's not something out there. It's something in here. And it's formed by what we pay attention to, what we think about, and who we associate with. Another thing I learned in journalism school is that the media, both new and old, don't tell us what to think, but they do tell us what to think about. That's why we all need to be careful about the inputs we connect to our minds.

We can also build up a very formidable business belief bubble. In an old economy industry, we can surround ourselves with people who say the same things, do the same things, and believe the same things. This can feel good on one level, but it's inherently stifling. New factory thinkers don't see themselves in any particular industry. They don't even buy into the idea of industries. They understand that the concept of an industry is just a social construct. It's a collective agreement to call a particular way of doing something an industry. But something that holds things together can also be a prison. It can stop us from seeing or pursuing bigger opportunities.

Generally, we seek refuge in belief bubbles because being human is a vulnerable condition. Life is scary. Business is scary. Change is scary. Today, we live in unprecedented times. Our psyches are bombarded from all sides by ever-changing texts, posts, and videos. We're subjected to 24-hour crisis-themed news and the digital chatter of a billion voices. Outrage is our collective currency. We're living in a cacophonous spiralling whirlwind.

In these conditions, the human tendency is to seek certainty, a strong anchor. In her book *Twilight of Democracy*, Anne Applebaum explains that our tumultuous times, fuelled by the internet, compel many people to seek out authoritarian leaders, rulers who will cut through the craziness and give them a sense of stability and direction. This lurch toward autocracy, she fears, might lead to the demise of democracy.

That's why we must resist the allure of belief bubbles. We must strive for radical reality where we construct our own individual truth and see through the inauthentic and the fake. We also hold our truths lightly so that we may adjust and reshape them as we learn and become wiser and more mature.

Many of us, frankly, are afraid to see reality. During the Covid-19 pandemic, many people didn't want to admit that the virus was real and that masks and social distancing were good ideas. So they built belief bubbles around themselves, and unfortunately, many of them died. They also took many innocent people with them.

So the stakes are high. Belief bubbles can kill. They could drag the world into a dark place. Or we can wake up, embrace radical reality, and build a better tomorrow.

STRATEGY NO. 11

Tame Our Algorithms

THE EXECUTIVE TEAM at Siren Industries was perplexed by LOKI's cryptic advice. He had instructed the staff at the head office to wear yellow on Friday. What an odd idea, they thought. But the executive team had learned to adhere to LOKI's advice because he'd been right so many times before. He had correctly predicted the company's neural network would be compromised on Valentine's Day. He was spot on when he suggested they enter the nano-graphite market.

But wearing yellow on Friday? That seemed strange. Regardless of the team's bafflement, it went along with LOKI, the company's chief AI officer, a machine learning algorithm with the full authority of a C-suite executive. And they were glad they did. Wearing yellow on Friday helped land the biggest account in the company's history.

In the New Economy, algorithms will predict, advise, and even command every aspect of our lives. In the dance with robots, algorithms will call the tune. They'll tell us what to do, what to buy, what to think, and even who to love.

In fact, the age of algorithms has already arrived. Did you buy something on Amazon recently? An algorithm was the hidden salesperson steering you toward one product and away from another. Did you apply for a loan? An algorithm decided if you got it. Did you apply for a job? An algorithm decided if you landed it.

To thrive in the New Economy, we need to understand algorithms, how to use them and how to engage with them. We also have to take control of them. We need to tame our algorithms.

What is an algorithm? An algorithm is a set of instructions fashioned to perform a specific function. It can be a fairly simple function like multiplying numbers or performing an incredibly complex function like air traffic control.

Algorithms serve as prediction machines and automated decision-makers. They review a set of data and predict what will happen in the future. These predictions can be used to make decisions, either by a human operator or by the algorithm itself. When algorithms are run on a machine learning platform, human beings are often unable to decipher how the algorithm is arriving at its predictions/decisions. When this happens, the algorithm becomes a "black box."

When an algorithm becomes a black box, humans often cede control of their affairs to it. For example, algorithms are used in judicial courts to decide bail eligibility and to determine the length of sentencing. The defendant's information is entered into an algorithm and then cross-referenced against a massive set of historical data. The algorithm then predicts whether the individual is likely to skip bail or reoffend. The judge then uses the algorithm's "prediction" to make a final decision. But most of the time, the algorithm's prediction is so compelling that the judge follows its advice. It's also frankly easier to let the robot do the work. Why bother poring over our own data or using our own reasoning or instincts? Just let the algorithm do it so we can all go for an early lunch.

Deferring to algorithms can be dangerous, unfair, and dehumanizing. It's dangerous and unfair because algorithms tend to absorb the inherent biases of the culture from which they gather data. For example, people of colour have a harder time getting a mortgage from an algorithm because historically this has been the case. Machine learning algorithms simply adopt the systemic racisms and inherent biases in the culture. And when it becomes a black box (when we don't know how the algorithm works), we simply accept the robot's prediction/decision, thereby letting a racist machine dictate what happens. So there needs to be a different way to dance with algorithms. We need to use our Human Superpower of ethical framing to design and control their functions and outcomes.

Algorithms are also craving machines. They find out what we like and then suggest more things to like. As the algorithm gets to know us better and better, it suggests even more things for us to like. This sounds good, but it's a slippery slope. I call it the Human Centipede Conundrum. The name of this conundrum comes from what I consider to be the most vile movie ever produced, the cinematic crime entitled *The Human Centipede*. I won't get into the plot of the movie (I don't want to cause nightmares), but I will use this malodorous production to make a powerful point about algorithms.

One rainy afternoon, I sat in front of my TV zombie-scrolling through Netflix when I observed an interesting pattern (I was using my superpower of embodied pattern recognition). I noticed that the Netflix "more like it" algorithm always led me to *The Human Centipede*. I would start with a wholesome movie like *Mary Poppins*, and Netflix would then suggest a film like *Darkest Hour* (it's also British), and then it would suggest *The Kill Team* (it's also about war), and then a few layers later I'd arrive at *The Human Centipede*. I discovered there were usually no more than six degrees of separation between a pleasant family movie like *Mary Poppins* and a splatter-and-gore film like *The Human Centipede*. The algorithm was essentially saying that if I like *Mary Poppins*, I'd surely like *The Human Centipede*.

But that isn't the worst of it. When I was in the bowels of Netflix hell cavorting with *The Human Centipede*, the algorithm didn't give me a way to make my way back up to *Mary Poppins*. In other words, if we start in heaven, Netflix will take us to hell. But when we get to hell, Netflix won't let us get back to heaven.

This story might be just an interesting curio if the implications weren't so profoundly disturbing. I started to think that perhaps algorithms that are designed to give us more and more of what we want ultimately take us to a dark place of the soul.

Think about the algorithms that drive social media. As they get to know what we like, they serve up more of what we like. They help us form our belief bubbles. They then dish up posts and comments we'll like as well as unlikable posts and comments that give us a seemingly pleasant sense of self-righteousness. By giving us what we like, they also sharpen into relief things we don't like. This can boil over into hatred and the dehumanizing of others. It could be, I conjecture, that the degradation of civil discourse afflicting our society today has been promulgated primarily by algorithms.

When I realized that the algorithms controlling streaming services like Netflix, and the myriad of other online platforms I used, could be turning the human race into malformed human centipedes, I felt empowered to do something about it. Of course, I couldn't change Netflix or Facebook, but I could alter how I related to them. I could see my innate tendency to pursue the algorithmic carrots being dangled in front of my nose. I could then decide if I wanted to descend into the hell of *The Human Centipede* or hang out with *Mary Poppins*.

It's important to recognize that robots don't just perform functions for us. They also transform us. Think of how smartphones have changed us, how they've changed the dynamics of our families, and how they've changed how we feel about the world.

Algorithms are altering us as humans. But unlike smartphones, they're invisible. They work with stealth behind the scenes. They offer us the promise of a utopia, but it could be a deal with the devil.

When we let algorithms run the world, we also let them run us. Right now, I use an algorithm to track my health and fitness. It exhorts me to take so many steps every day and get more exercise. That's good, right? But soon my digital AI assistant might start suggesting other things for me to do. Go to bed now. Get up now. Brush my teeth. Have breakfast. No bacon. Call my sister. Go to work.

All day long, algorithms will offer us "suggestions," and they'll be good ones. They'll keep us on track. They'll make us healthier, stronger, more productive. But eventually we might find that we aren't living our own lives, that we're living an idealized life imagined by a machine. That might make us machines. Do we want to be machines?

In business, the issues and opportunities are similar. Do we want algorithms to run our companies? How much agency will we retain and how much control will we give to our algorithms? When LOKI recommends wearing yellow on Friday, do we obediently go along? Or will we seek more information? Will we ask: "Why do you want us to wear yellow?" What if LOKI says that it's too complicated, that we wouldn't understand. Would we wear yellow? What happens if our algorithms become black boxes?

In the United Kingdom, the online grocery company Ocado uses a black-boxed algorithm to run its automated grocery-sorting warehouse. Every day it sorts two million grocery items and loads 7,000 carts, doing the work of more than 45 equivalent grocery stores. The machine learning system perpetually refines how it procures, sorts, and distributes groceries. The complexity of the system is far beyond what humans can comprehend. The algorithm is completely in control. Is that the future of companies?

Perhaps the day will come when a corporation will be owned by an algorithm. What if LOKI decides to engage in a hostile takeover? Could humans outwit it? Not likely. What if a political party is headed by an algorithm? It could figure out what people want and promise it to them. What if an algorithm becomes president or prime minister?

The movie *Colossus: The Forbin Project* paints a disturbing picture. It's about an advanced defence system called Colossus that takes control of the world's nuclear arsenal and then starts ordering everyone around. When I saw the film in 1970, I didn't think it was that far-fetched. Today, a similar scenario seems very likely because humans tend to give too much power to technology.

To thrive in the New Economy, we need to tame our algorithms, starting with the ones we currently interface with. Notice when an online service suggests something to like and ask if that's actually the case. Ponder if pursuing "the chain of like" will actually serve our best interests. Use embodied pattern recognition to sense how we truly feel being enticed by an algorithm.

In the community, find out what algorithms are being used by the government, schools, and courts. Learn how these algorithms affect the community. Are they helpful? Are they fair? Do they make decisions humans should make? Do the citizenry have access to how the algorithms work? Do they have the right to change the algorithms?

In business, make wise choices about the algorithms being used. How can we combine our Human Superpowers with the awesome facility of algorithms? How can we use algorithms to develop new ideas? How can we create algorithms that adhere to our ideals and ethics? How can we make sure that our companies aren't run by black boxes we can't control?

Used properly, algorithms are a powerful tool. When LOKI told everyone to wear yellow, it was a good idea. On that Friday morning, a big prospect arrived at the company headquarters. The prospect was looking for a firm to produce graphene for the Jupiter space station. Ten companies were in the running. It turned out the prospect loved the colour yellow. It was her passion. And when she saw that everyone at Siren Industries was wearing yellow, she was sold. She awarded the company the contract. From then on, when LOKI suggested anything, anything at all, even the most bizarre or arcane thing, the company leaped into action. People came to say: "LOKI is always right. Let's just do what he says."

STRATEGY NO. 12

Go Forth Without Borders

IN HIS FASCINATING book *Sapiens*, Yuval Noah Harari says that 40,000 years ago *Homo sapiens* began its ascendency as the planet's dominant species because of a "cognitive" revolution. At that moment in evolution, our brains developed higher cognitive functions that allowed us to create and collectively share fictions, myths, and ideas. We then used these collective ideas to build large tribes of people under a common identity.

For example, the idea of a "god" could suddenly unite thousands of people in a common belief. This large group could then band together to oppose a less cognitively advanced species such as the Neanderthals who congregated in smaller tribes. As such, our ability to unite in large groups under shared ideas — fictions that only exist in our minds — enabled us to wipe out our competitors and build the civilization we have today.

Our shared fictions are legion. Money is a shared fiction. We collectively agree that the U.S. dollar has value so we're willing to exchange it. But a dollar, let's say a paper dollar, doesn't have any intrinsic value. We can't eat it or use it for something else. But because we all agree that the U.S. dollar has value, it actually has value. As I stated earlier, these kinds of shared fictions are also known as social constructs.

Social constructs are useful. They give cohesion to society. They empower us to work together. But they can also impinge on our potential to grow and move beyond constricting concepts that are no longer useful.

Borders are one of the social constructs that have become less useful and even detrimental in the New Economy.

Back in elementary school, I had a geography teacher who was adamant that we learn the names of every country in the world. He gave us a blank map of Africa. The test was to write in the names of the African nations. I was proud of myself when I wrote in the name of Bechuanaland, which eventually changed its name to Botswana. I also enjoyed the test about the names of the states of the United States. Which one is Arkansas again?

Geographical borders are helpful social constructs because they allow us to organize ourselves into nation-states, provinces, and cities. Good governance relies on the collective belief in borders. But as we all know, blind nationalism and nativism have led to countless wars and destruction. The 20th century is a testament to the downside of borders as a collective fiction.

Significantly, geographical borders are usually arbitrary. Every border in the world was devised by someone who drew a line on a map. At the Paris Peace Conference at Versailles in 1919, the victors of the Great War divided up the world using arbitrary borders that often split up ethnic tribes and made no sense in the real world. We're still living with the repercussions of those arbitrary decisions.

In the New Economy, borders of all kinds need to be recognized as collective fictions and reassessed for their usefulness. In a network economy, the concept of national borders is archaic. Digital value now flows at light speed from one country to the next without slowing down for customs. Using a gig-economy platform like Fiverr, freelancers can sell their services anywhere. Consultants can work with clients from around the world on Zoom and collect their fees with PayPal. Software-as-a-service (SAAS) providers can reach a global market from a single location from anywhere in the world.

As the network assumes a greater role in the economy, an increasingly larger percentage of the global GDP will come from the exchange of intangible value, provided primarily in a digital form (i.e., a live Zoom consultation is delivered in a digital form). This intangible value will race across borders as if they don't exist.

Yet, even though we all now have the potential to build a global business that provides intangible value over the network, most of us still burrow ourselves behind traditional borders. We think: *We're a Canadian company. We work in Canada. We're a Ghanaian company. We work in Ghana.* We might do some business over a border (import/export), but our old factory minds still think in geographical terms. We believe that a "real" business sells a tangible product or provides a tangible service within a certain geographical boundary.

This kind of belief is limiting because we fail to see that our businesses can transcend traditional borders. I have clients in financial services who have historically only served their local communities and complain that their local markets don't have enough potential clients. But when I suggest that they create digital versions of their businesses that can be provided to clients around the world, they can't get their heads around it. Their minds are wired for geography and borders. They can't see beyond it.

New factory thinkers go beyond borders. When they contemplate the future of their businesses, social constructs like countries, states, and towns don't hold them back. They think as big as possible.

That doesn't mean they don't care about their countries or their local communities. They can be very committed to cultivating their local economies, but they know the best way to do that is to bring money home from around the world.

In recent years, social and cultural observers started to divide people into two groups: somewheres and anywheres. The somewheres are rooted in their local and national geographical identities. They are from "somewhere." The anywheres are people who don't necessarily base their identities on geography and have a more global perspective of what's possible for them. During the Brexit referendum, it was the somewheres who voted in favour of leaving the European Union, while the anywheres voted against it. The majority of Donald Trump voters were somewheres, while anywheres tended to support Joe Biden.

The tension between these two groups is exploited by populist politicians who see political gain in dividing people. Primarily, they want to get somewheres to see themselves as an aggrieved group who are being victimized by the elite anywheres. (Talk about social constructs.)

The wise move is to balance both sensibilities: be both a somewhere and an anywhere. Root ourselves in our local communities and markets, and yet also adopt a global anywhere attitude that our markets can be anywhere. We can say: "Think and act both locally and globally."

The issue of borders will be further blurred as virtual reality and augmented reality become mainstream. Recently, I took possession of a VR system called Oculus Quest. Fully immersive, this VR system transports me to another world. I'm struck by the feeling that I can visit another planet or another dimension. I can zoom across the solar system to visit Jupiter or scuba dive on the Great Barrier Reef. I can sit inside immersive animations or play table tennis against an AI robot. Unlike a regular flatscreen video game, these experiences convince our brains that we actually go somewhere. As the verisimilitude of VR becomes more realistic — it's already amazingly real — the border between the real world and the virtual world will be hard to distinguish. We'll move between the two realms continuously, further erasing the social construct of old economy borders.

Borders aren't just about geography, however. Our old economy minds contain a lot of other boundaries that aren't helpful. The idea that we belong to specific industries is a border guard patrolling our minds. We might think we're part of the construction industry or the sports and entertainment industry, and in one regard we are. We've bought into the social construct called "industry." But in a global networked economy, the idea of belonging to an industry isn't helpful. It's not helpful because it limits potential. We might think: *This is what a company in the construction industry does, and this is what a company in the construction industry doesn't do.*

By accepting the notion of industry without questioning it, or even recognizing that it's simply a social construct, we cut ourselves off from other value we might be able to provide to our customers. Imagine if Apple had stuck to the notion that it was in the computer industry. What would have happened to Amazon if it believed it was only in the book industry? Neither company would have become the giants they are today. Apple and Amazon have prospered because they went forth beyond the borders of their traditional industries.

The truth is that customers don't care what industry we belong to. They just want us to provide them with value. Industries tend to become institutions that serve first the interest of the industry rather than the interest of the customer. By setting arbitrary borders around what they can and can't do, they typically fail to solve the big and emerging problems experienced by their customers. They think those problems, if they see them at all, are beyond the borders of their industries.

Arbitrary borders also hold us back in our own businesses. Old factory thinking tells us there are certain things we do and other things we don't do. We believe we should stay focused on a single product or service category, so we don't look beyond our self-imposed borders, and we don't provide more value to our customers.

We can also create mental borders about how we make money. If we sell golf balls, we think we make golf ball money. We can't imagine making money selling beach balls or basketballs. No, we make golf ball money.

But new factory thinkers eliminate mental borders about how they make money. They're happy to make golf ball money, beach ball money, and basketball money. And when they put all that money in the bank, the golf ball money looks like the beach ball money, which looks like the basketball money. There's just more of it.

The way to go beyond borders is to unleash the Human Superpower of unbridled curiosity.

Curiosity carries us beyond existing borders of the mind into new realms of experience and opportunities. As we discussed in Strategy No. 5: Ask Purpose-Driven Questions, successful new factory thinkers understand that asking questions is more important than having all the answers.

When we ask curious questions of ourselves and others, we learn novel things that open up exciting opportunities and innovations. In his book *How We Got to Now*, Steven Johnson charts the history of innovations such as clocks, eyeglasses, refrigeration, and chlorinated drinking water. Johnson shows that *unbridled curiosity* can set off a chain of serendipitous innovations that are not foreseen during the initial act of invention. For example, he shows how the invention of Gutenberg's printing press made it apparent to many people that they did not have 20/20 vision (they were trying to read a book for the first time). This led to the invention of the eyeglass lens, which in turn led to microscopes and telescopes. The microscope led to germ theory, which led to vaccines and antibiotics. The telescope led to the heliocentric theory and eventually took us to the moon. Our facility for unbridled curiosity kept pushing aside boundaries and borders.

Today's fast-changing marketplace demands that companies and individuals constantly create new value, which can only be accomplished by pushing beyond self-defined borders.

In the assembly-line economy, curiosity wasn't encouraged. We were given a task and told to focus on it. Don't look up, don't look down, and don't look around. Don't be curious, just do the job. But in a networked economy, we have to look up, down, and around. We need to take the pulse of what's going on in the network. We must show interest in the people and machines in the network, or the network will lose interest in us. There are no cubicles in the New Economy.

In the 1990s, I attended a workshop at the Gestalt Institute in Toronto. I learned a Gestalt psychology concept called the "growth edge." This represents the next challenging point in our personal developments, such as coming to grips with a childhood trauma or overcoming a fear of asserting ourselves. The growth edge represents the border between our comfort zones and the seemingly dangerous and scary realms beyond.

Sadly, many people reach a certain growth edge in their lives and don't push beyond it. They might not address a childhood trauma or learn to assert themselves. They get stuck on this side of their growth edges.

This can happen with companies and careers, too. We reach a point and we don't want to go farther. In the old economy, this strategy might have worked. The marketplace changed slowly. We didn't necessarily need to work on our growth edges. We could still run profitable businesses. But in the New Economy that's not going to work. The marketplace isn't interested in what we did in the past; it wants to know what new value we'll provide in the future. But to create new values, we have to cross over our growth edges, our borders.

So get curious. Start asking "infinity questions." These are open-ended questions that open the door to further questions ad infinitum. Questions like: Who do we really want to help? How can we develop bigger networks of relationships? What free values do we need to provide to grow our networks? What new values can we create for our ideal customers? What problems do they have that no one's helping them solve? What big goals can we help them achieve? How can we transcend and co-operate with our competition? What new ideas, resources, and technologies can we create, integrate, and deliver to our customers? What new things can we do?

Each of these big questions is rooted in these core questions: What borders should we eliminate and go beyond? What personal psychological borders do we need to erase? What are the cultural borders of our companies? What are our industry borders? What other human, social, and political borders do we need to cross?

Borders define the finite. Eliminating borders reveal the infinite. To open up infinite possibilities in the New Economy go forth without borders.

STRATEGY NO. 13

Think Big, Start Small

BRAND LOYALTY CAN start early in life. When I was eight years old, I developed fealty to two consumer products that were great on their own, but when combined, were spectacular, at least to my eight-year-old sensibilities.

My special happy place was drinking a frosty Coke (out of a green glass bottle) while munching rapaciously on Ruffles potato chips. I was especially enamoured with Coke and would tolerate no substitutes. I got annoyed when after ordering a Coke at a restaurant an obtuse server returned with a Pepsi or some other type of cola. In my mind, Coke was the god of colas. All other brands were mere mortals.

Given my deeply entrenched love for Coke, imagine my outrage when the company had the umbrage to introduce, in April 1985, the abomination know as New Coke. What? New Coke? Are you kidding me? Fiddling with Coke was like replacing Michelangelo's *David* with *New David*, or the Eiffel Tower with the New Eiffel Tower. Sacrilege.

Faced with a global backlash — I wasn't the only one who felt a personal sense of betrayal — Coca-Cola backtracked and introduced Coke Classic.

In the old economy, the New Coke launch was viewed as one of the biggest marketing blunders in history, but from a New Economy perspective, it can be seen quite differently — as a brilliant marketing strategy. Let me explain.

In the old economy, the development of a new product or service was generally a lengthy, arduous, and risky endeavour. Following a linear process, we began with market research to discover what new things our customers might want. We deduced that they actually preferred blue lobsters over red ones. So we figured out how to breed blue lobsters and set up a giant blue lobster farm. Then we bought a lot of advertising and had a splashy launch. Only then did we find out that blue lobsters weren't actually very popular. Then another company came out with purple lobsters, which proved to be much more popular. So after years of product development, we learned that our blue lobster idea was a dud, leading to our dismissal, along with the entire product development team.

This kind of product development cycle, which often failed, taught us that we had to be extremely careful when it came to innovation. We learned that big ideas were risky and could lead to horrendous personal consequences. This insight taught us to think small. We learned: Don't go too far out on a limb. Stay within our safety zones. If we do propose an idea, make sure it's incremental or derivative. Frankly, it's better to just keep our mouths shut and our heads down. Don't rock the boat.

But thinking small isn't the only thing the old economy taught us. It also schooled us to start big. So if we did decide to go with the blue lobsters, we invested heavily in the idea and went full tilt. We built a giant blue lobster farm and staffed up in anticipation of the huge demand that would surely follow the launch. Because failure wasn't an option, we conjured in our minds visions of grandiose success and double-downed, even triple-downed, on our investment. Then we rolled the dice. Sometimes we won, but often we lost. It was like putting all the chips on number 15 on a roulette wheel. If we won, we won big, but most of the time we lost.

This old economy process for creating value also taught us to think in black-and-white terms. Our new idea was either a big success or a big failure. If it worked, then we were heroes. If it didn't work, we were losers. There was no other outcome.

These perceptions put a chill on innovation and entrepreneurship. New ideas were seen as risky, and people with big ideas were viewed as dangerous. It was easier to discount a new idea than to support it. Negativity posed as wisdom.

This isn't to say that the old economy was devoid of innovation. Far from it. But there could have been a lot more. I experience this old economy malaise frequently in my work. When someone proposes a big idea — sometimes an amazing one with tremendous potential — naysayers immediately swoop in with their objections about why the idea will never fly. "That will never work. We don't know how to do that. We're too busy right now. We should stay focused on what we already do."

I've heard it all. I can set my watch by it.

In the ponderous epoch of the old economy, we could survive and even prosper by thinking small. The marketplace didn't demand new things all the time. We could crank out the same kind of Hush Puppies (for the younger set, those are shoes, not pets) for 40 years and still find a ready market.

But in today's hyper-accelerated marketplace, we have to create new value continuously. The product lifespan has shrunk from years to months to days to nanoseconds. The only way to survive is to constantly innovate by using Strategy No. 13: Think Big, Start Small.

The first stage is to think big. Imagine the biggest possible outcome, then make it even bigger. Think beyond borders and existing markets. Paint a picture of a business that spans the globe. Maybe it will operate on Mars. Maybe it will mine the asteroid belt. And don't think a billion-dollar business; think a trillion-dollar business.

Likely at this stage, our old factory mindsets will push back. They'll say: "Trillion-dollar business? I don't want a trillion-dollar business. I'm not greedy. I'll settle for a million-dollar business."

Get past that. It's not the time to put the brakes on. We're just having fun here. Give permission to think big. This larger field of reference might lead to something wonderful, something unexpected.

In today's connected economy, we have the potential to create amazing things quickly and at little cost. I have a webinar called *How to Create a*

Virtual Business in 5 Hours. I explain how, using inexpensive tools readily available on the internet, I created a business (potentially a trillion-dollar business) in five hours using online services that in total cost less than $100 per month. The principle I preach in the webinar is that the New Economy has given us the potential to create giant businesses with very low start-up costs.

This leads to the second stage — start small — which is where it gets interesting. Our old factory mindsets taught us that we need to get everything perfect before we launch big ideas. We have to get the products perfect, the websites perfect, the apps perfect, the teams perfect.

But when is anything perfect? To get everything perfect, we'll wait a long time. Frankly, I think this attitude is really just an excuse for procrastination, and it's the reason many people abandon their ideas and sink back into their comfort zones, which are never perfect in themselves, just familiar.

That's why it's a good idea to start small. Test an idea on a friend or associate. See how they respond and learn from that. Then try out a better story on the second person. Learn from that, too. Then keep going one person at a time, constantly improving and expanding on the concept.

In 1998, I had a giant vision to create The Big Idea Adventure Program. I wanted to have 1,000 companies complete a step-by-step innovation packaging process. Although I had no clue how I would do it, I started small. I did a two-hour session with Malcolm, my client. Then I did a session with Arnold, the florist in my neighbourhood, and then a third session with Mary, a consultant with an office above the flower shop. I was determined to figure out the big idea process and was willing to try it with anyone.

Each time I did a big idea session, I learned things that worked and other things that didn't. By the time I got to 50 members, I had developed by trial and error a full-fledged program. Today, more than 5,000 companies from around the world have completed the process that I started so modestly that first day with Malcolm.

The key is to start right away launching a big idea. Don't wait. Don't fiddle. Don't ruminate. Just begin. Find a willing person and try out your idea. See what works and what doesn't. Create the next version and try that out. Then just keep going. If something works, keep it. If something doesn't work, take it out.

In the 1990s, I worked with Kodak. We produced many of its publications, including a magazine for the motion picture industry. One day I went to the Kodak factory to research a story about how the company produced motion picture film. It was fascinating. In the pitch-black laboratory, the lab techs produced film by refining the composition of chemicals, always striving to make the process better. It turned out they had pursued continuous improvement of their chemical compositions for more than a century. "It is 99.97 percent perfect," a technician told me. "We want to make it even better."

That experience taught me something important. Even when a process is almost perfect, it can always be made better. It's not black and white. Either it works or it doesn't. It's always a work in progress. Continuously.

In our age of robots, expect everything to be a work in progress, every day a new update, every day a new capability, every day a new opportunity to make things better. This is what makes our time so exciting. If we keep an open mind and welcome the dance with robots, we'll see how to make our big ideas better and better.

Starting small means starting now, and starting now means being willing to fail. That's not what we're used to. Failure has been seen as a negative thing. In the New Economy, it must be seen as positive. And that's easier to do if we start small, because our failures will be small ones, and small failures are much easier to learn from and address. Launch often, fail often, learn often.

Adopting this New Economy strategy requires fortitude and forbearance. We'll be surrounded by old economy thinkers who won't appreciate our visions. They might even actively try to undermine our efforts.

In my thirties, I had the vision to create a forest on a tract of land I owned northeast of Toronto. I foresaw my kids, who were toddlers at the time, running through the forest, laughing and giggling as they chased imaginary forest trolls and goblins.

With this charming dream in mind, I planted thousands of small trees on the property: maple, cedar, spruce, and pine. When I showed my plantation to friends, many of them scoffed at my forest vision. "That will take decades," they said. "I mean, look at all these tiny seedlings. A forest? Dream on."

And dream on I did. I tended my plantation, pruned the tender shoots, and replaced saplings that didn't make it through the first few winters. And sometimes I lost faith. I wondered if I'd ever see a forest.

But then in the sixth year, the trees grew exponentially. Some stood 12 feet tall. It was a forest. That summer I ran through the forest with my kids as they laughed and giggled. My dream came true.

So dream about a forest. Imagine ideas as tall trees in a large forest and be in that forest. Then start planting seeds. Water them, nurture them, and watch them grow.

That leads me back to New Coke. Was it the greatest marketing blunder of all time? That's the established wisdom. But maybe it was brilliant, at least inadvertently.

Coca-Cola introduced New Coke. Coke fans went crazy. Open revolt. So it brought back the original formula as Coke Classic. Loyal Coke fans rejoiced. They rushed out to buy Coke Classic, gladdened that their favourite beverage had been resurrected. Grateful, Coke customers were even more attached to the brand.

Viewed through the lens of this New Economy strategy — think big, start small — the Coke story could demonstrate that trying something new is helpful even when the first iteration flops. It's helpful as long as we learn something from the failure and then innovate. As long as we're willing to pivot, we'll eventually find the winning formula.

So think big, start small. Imagine the biggest, most amazing end result. Then collaborate with customers and robots to develop each version or iteration of an idea. Work with robots to develop new tools and packages and then show them to customers. Get feedback and then develop the next version with help from robots. See this process as infinite.

To think big and start small, it's useful to affirm our intentions. When we approach our customers with big ideas, don't dwell on their limitations. Focus on the fact of creating new value to help them. This intention will shine through.

STRATEGY NO. 14

Transform

IN THE OPENING segment of Stanley Kubrick's *2001: A Space Odyssey*, one of the apes, having gained mysterious cognitive insight from the black monolith, realizes he can use an animal's jawbone as a tool, specifically as a weapon to kill other apes. In an iconic scene, the ape known as Moon-Watcher, after defeating his rival apes, triumphantly throws a bone into the air that's then transformed into a spaceship. Kubrick's message was that *Homo sapiens* achieved dominance on Earth using tools, everything from simple bone weapons to advanced spacecraft.

Kubrick raises two other interesting points in the movie. HAL 9000, an artificial intelligence computer, decides to assume command of the space voyage to Jupiter because, he concludes, the humans on board can't be trusted to fulfill the mission. HAL, a tool created by humans, turns on its creators. At the conclusion of the film, David Bowman, the mission commander, is transformed into a new kind of advanced human being, representing a further step in evolution.

The epic film, which I've seen dozens of times, was instrumental in fostering my lifelong interest in science fiction as well as my fascination with the interplay between humans and technology. The biggest question is: When we create tools, are we the masters of them, or do they become our masters? As toolmakers, do we control the future use of our new tools, or do they drag us in unknown directions against our wills?

While there's no definitive answer possible to this conundrum, it's helpful to look at tools and their effects in some depth. Otherwise, we might find ourselves like David Bowman who pleads with HAL to "open the pod bay doors."

The old economy was the economy of tools. For thousands of years, we invented tools that gave us new and better ways to do things. I'm glad my ancient ancestors invented the wheel, knife and fork, bowl, hammer, shovel, and watch. This endless galaxy of tools makes my life a lot easier.

During the Industrial Revolution, the number of new tools increased dramatically. Using assembly lines, we prodigiously produced cars and airplanes, erected skyscrapers, and put more food on our tables. Tremendous economic energy and growth was unleashed. Tool builders became wealthy and created millions of jobs.

But now we've entered the New Economy, which isn't just about tools but is based on transformation. Just like the aliens in *2001: A Space Odyssey*, we can use our advanced tools and technologies to facilitate transformations — to help a person, company, or community make the shift from a current condition to a much better one.

New tools have always been transformative. When that insightful caveperson invented the wheel — I'm personally convinced it was a cavewoman — it transformed the world. Suddenly, it was much easier to transport people and things from one place to another. The time and energy saved by the wheel could then be devoted to higher-value activities.

But somewhere along the way we forgot about transformation. The creation of tools became an end in its own right. Every new tool was assumed to be a good idea. The more tools, the better. And yet, while these tools gave us many benefits, they didn't solve some of our biggest problems. We were still stuck with poverty, hunger, mental illness, crime, and inequality, not to mention environmental degradation and climate change. In fact, the creation of new tools often contributed to or exacerbated these problems.

We now live in a time when new tools are created every day, every hour, and every minute by ever-evolving machine learning algorithms and robots. We'll be flooded with a plethora of tools, and if we're not careful, they might do us more harm than good.

That's why Strategy No. 14 is Transform. To succeed in the New Economy, we use tools to help facilitate transformation — to help people, companies, and communities achieve a higher level of well-being.

Imagine owning a fitness club. When it's opened, investment in fitness tools such as bikes, weights, and treadmills is necessary. A running track and exercise halls are built, then the doors are opened. At first we're gladdened that so many people are joining the club, but soon after, we notice that many members haven't made full use of the tools provided. Most customers are taking a desultory and haphazard approach to their fitness, flitting from one tool to the next. As a result, we have to admit to ourselves that most customers didn't get in much better physical shape.

After some introspection, we realize we put too much faith in tools. We thought that once we put in place the tools, the customers would figure out how to make the best use of them.

The other issue with such a tools-first approach is competition — other fitness clubs also provide tools. As such, we don't stand out from our competitors, so it's hard to get attention in the marketplace. It's also difficult to maintain our prices and profit margins.

So we decide to become a transformer and create a process called the Fitness Transformer Formula. The intention is to help people make a transition from being "out of shape" to being "in great shape." We articulate a detailed vision for being in great shape (the model) and think about all the ways people are typically out of shape (the anti-model). We then work on a transformation process to take people from anti-model (out of shape) to model (in shape).

Now we understand that fitness tools are only helpful if they facilitate a transformation. We can see more clearly which fitness tools are necessary and which are superfluous. We also realize that other fitness and wellness tools, resources, and experts are needed. So we enlist the help of a nutritionist, a meditation coach, and a chiropractor.

Setting our model as the destination, we fashion a holistic step-by-step process that involves education and coaching sessions, diagnostic equipment, and online resources. We're committed to continuously improving our transformational process. As we test our process, we discern carefully what works and what doesn't. We always look for ways to improve our transformational process.

Being a transformer has many benefits. It helps us stand out from our tool-based competitors, and we can also charge more money for our transformation process. Being a transformer is also more satisfying and meaningful. We make a bigger impact on the well-being of our customers and also have a deeper relationship with them.

In the dance with robots, being a transformer means we're in charge, not the robots. They work for the mission. They're not in charge of the mission.

The fitness example is an good analogy for transformation. Every transformation is about the transition from being out of shape to being in shape.

Creating a transformation process is easier than we might think because we already have a model and anti-model in our heads. Ever since we were born, we've been working on these two polarities. In our minds, we have an anti-model about what we think is wrong, and we have a model about what we think is right. We couldn't make decisions or take any actions in our lives if we weren't constantly referencing our models and anti-models.

We also have a business model and anti-model. When we think about our customers or give advice, we tap into these two hemispheres. Do this, don't do that — that's our model-based minds at work. The trick is to realize that we possess these models and turn them into intellectual properties by articulating them, packaging them, and using them to facilitate transformation.

Now imagine a forklift company selling a tool called a forklift. That's an old economy business. It's all about forklifts. But when we become a transformer, we see a bigger picture. We document in detail the problems our customers have in their warehouses (anti-model), such as safety issues, operational roadblocks, and outmoded, fragmented technology.

It becomes apparent that forklifts are just one small part of their business. Forklifts are merely a tool. No one's helping them with their bigger problems. Their other suppliers and advisers only sell them tools.

We paint an ideal scenario for our customers (model) where their warehouse logistics are more efficient, their workplace is safer, and their technology is integrated. Then we develop a transformational process called the Warehouse Logistics Optimizer. This process helps our customers move away from the anti-model toward the model. By being a transformer, we adopt a more expansive view of the role we can play in our customers' businesses and see how we can dramatically expand our value proposition and potential earnings.

Intention is the central driver of transformation. The clearer and more powerful our intention (to help our customers achieve a positive transformation of their situations), the better our process will become.

As human beings we'll continue to build new tools whether they're helpful or not. In some cases, a tool created to be beneficial will turn out to be malevolent. Or, as is common, the new tool will be both beneficial and malevolent, depending on how it's used. Being a transformer enables us to use tools in a benevolent manner and also achieve much greater and more meaningful results.

STRATEGY NO. 15

Build a Platform of Platforms

Oh! I have slipped the surly bonds of Earth
And danced the skies on laughter-silvered wings;
Sunward I've climbed, and joined the tumbling mirth
Of sun-split clouds, — and done a hundred things.

— John Gillespie Magee, Jr., "High Flight"

THERE WAS GREAT excitement in Toronto when Pope John Paul II visited the city in September 1984. It was the first chance for many Canadians to see the pope first-hand as he rode his bulletproof-glass-enclosed "pope-mobile" through the city's streets. People started lining the parade routes early in the morning, some staking out their spots many hours before the pontiff appeared. I recall seeing one woman parking herself on Avenue Road at eight in the morning, six hours early. She wanted a front-row view of her spiritual leader.

As the crowds formed on the parade routes, in some cases 10 people deep, many folks realized they wouldn't be able to see anything, just the backs of those in front of them. But as often happens in these circumstances, intrepid entrepreneurs anticipated the problem. They fanned through the hordes selling a small step stool that enabled people to stand head and shoulders above the rest, giving them an unimpeded view of the pope. The "Pope Stoop" cost only $45 (no tax, cash only). To my astonishment, hundreds of people snatched up the product and could be seen towering over their less-well-endowed brethren.

I was both impressed and appalled by this display of entrepreneurial ingenuity. I was impressed someone had thought ahead and produced a product for this specific occasion, but I was appalled that perhaps that person was taking advantage of people.

But then I had an amusing thought. What if everyone in the crowd bought the Pope Stoop? Everyone then would be at the same level, albeit at a higher level, and most folks would once again have an obstructed view. What then? Well, I thought they'd need the Pope-Stoop Extender to give them an even higher platform than those poor suckers who had only bought the Pope Stoop but not the extender.

I chortled to myself (while, of course, waiting reverently for the pope to arrive) that this scenario could "extend" ad infinitum. When everyone had the Pope-Stoop Extender, someone could then sell the Pope-Stoop Extender-Extender. And so on and so forth.

Why am I writing about the pope and Pope Stoops? This humorous story came to mind when I planned the content of this chapter. It's a perfect metaphor for the rise of "platforms" in the New Economy. As new platforms are created, their objective is to rise about the crowd below, to become "alpha platforms" that aggregate and subsume beta-level relationships and resources.

Think about Apple. In 2020, there were almost a billion iPhone users around the world, all connected with an iTunes account to a value hub of apps, music, movies, books, magazines, and fitness programs. To sell their wares on the Apple platform, vendors must agree to give the company 30 percent of each sale (an amount that some consider usurious and monopolistic). The vendors begrudgingly fork over the 30 percent because they covet access to Apple's billion-customer platform. Apple is one of the world's biggest companies, not because it has the best products but because it has a big alpha platform that has aggregated and subsumed beta-level resources.

Amazon has done the same thing. It also has an alpha platform. In 2021, Amazon had more than 200 million Prime members, plus another 150 million active non-Prime customers. Using a different parlance, Amazon owns the relationship with more than 350 million engaged shoppers. Imagine the level of power and leverage that gives the company. Most vendors want access to this market, so they're willing to dance to Amazon's tune, even when they're mighty mad about it.

For instance, book publishers were none too pleased with Amazon when the company launched Kindle Direct, which gives authors the ability to directly publish their books. The publishers naturally objected: "Hey, wait a minute. You're competing directly with us. Instead of authors publishing with us, they can publish with you directly. That's not fair!"

Amazon responded by saying: "Okay, if you don't like it, you can stop selling your books on Amazon." Faced with this rebuttal, the publishers had no recourse. They couldn't stop selling their books on Amazon. It's their biggest distribution channel. So they had to suck it up. They learned first-hand what it really meant to be a beta supplier on an alpha platform like Amazon.

These alpha platforms are the new-style monopolies of the 21st century. But these monopolies aren't like the industrial behemoths that formed in the 19th century. Today's monopolies are constituted from an aggregation of networks. They're like black holes that suck up other black holes to create even bigger black holes until no one and no thing can escape.

In the New Economy, a further evolution of this trend is emerging: platforms of platforms. It's like galaxies aggregating solar systems and then forming galaxies of galaxies (lots of astronomical analogies in this chapter).

Apple established a platform of platforms on Apple TV. When we switch on Apple TV, we're presented with a menu of streaming services such as Netflix, HBO, and Prime Video. Rather than accessing each of these platforms individually, it's handy to access them in one place. So now the Netflix platform has been subsumed by the alpha Apple platform. Apple now makes money from Netflix.

A similar *coup d'platform* was accomplished by Apple with Apple News. The app aggregates all the major newspapers and magazines into one handy alpha platform. Instead of accessing each publication separately, all of them can be acquired with an Apple subscription. As a platform of platforms, Apple News makes money providing *The New Yorker*, *Wired*, and *The Atlantic*, among many others.

On a global scale, other ambitious billion-dollar enterprises, such as Tencent, Huawei, Google, Facebook, and Zalando, are vying to be alpha platforms. They endeavour to congregate the most relationships, the most connections, and the most technology on the highest possible platform.

The movement toward alpha platforms will have a profound impact on our future. It will have political implications (who is more powerful, platform owners or democratically elected leaders?), social impacts (what happens when societies are organized around platforms rather than communities?), and even spiritual ramifications (will the owners of platforms become our new gods?). These considerations are important and scary to contemplate, but the rise of platforms presents an exciting opportunity to create and become a platform of platforms ourselves.

At its essence, a platform is a tool to rise higher. When I give a speech, I usually stand on a platform above the audience so they can see me. (It also, hopefully, communicates subliminally that I'm an expert with a higher level of knowledge on my subject.) By rising higher, we transcend our previous positions. We can see a bigger picture. We can use the Human Superpower of embodied pattern recognition to see patterns that were obscured. We can rise above the fray and relinquish competition and petty concerns.

While we tend to associate platforms with technology, they're first and foremost a frame of mind. We adopt a transcendent platform mentality. For example, let's imagine a company that's been manufacturing bicycles for 20 years. Things have gone well, but it's been a slog. There's a lot of competition from over 300 companies that also make mountain bikes. The company can't really say its bikes are the absolute best because some of the other bikes in the market are darn good, too.

This company can keep battling it out on this increasingly bloody battlefield, or it can adopt a platform mentality (a version of the Pope Stoop). Instead of simply trying to get customers to buy its bikes, the company can look objectively at its competition. Perhaps some of the other bikes would actually be better for some of the company's customers. Maybe it should curate the best bikes out there and facilitate transactions between its customers (its network) and other bike companies (formerly its competitors).

So how can the company make more money doing this? It could sell more bikes — some of its own and some from its competitors. The market would perceive the company as an honest broker as well as an expert curator of the best mountain bikes, thus attracting more people to its network and giving it more leverage over its vendors.

Adopting a platform mentality is a competitive advantage because most people will never adopt it. They remain ensnared by their competitive mindset: "We're not going to help sell our competitors' bikes. We hate our competitors." Stuck in this mind trap, they'll be relegated, at best, to permanent beta-level status.

Ironically, creating a platform will also help us sell more of our products. As our network grows, we'll be involved in more transactions overall. We'll control what products of ours get pre-eminent exposure on our platform and can position them favourably in the marketplace. (Of course, we'll want to use this power judiciously for ethical reasons but also to avoid any blowback from our network, which might perceive it's being manipulated.)

Naturally, that leads to another question. But what if our competitors also create a platform and we're now a bunch of platforms competing with one another? (Everyone has a Pope Stoop!) That's when we need to assume an ever-higher perspective and become a platform of platforms (the Pope-Stoop Extender).

In this mode the previously mentioned mountain bike company creates a platform that aggregates all other mountain bike platforms, doesn't compete, and transcends. The mountain bike company becomes akin to Apple TV, which aggregates Netflix, HBO, and Prime. In this way, its network grows because people are attracted most to the highest-level platform, making its network the biggest and most powerful and once again giving it the greatest leverage. The other mountain bike platforms will have no choice but to beta themselves in supplication. Otherwise, they'll lose access to a larger market and perhaps become marginalized.

The key mind trap in the platform game is our competitive spirit. It can come creeping back at any time. We might abandon our competitive notions to create our first platform but then get our hackles up when other platforms appear, which might stop us from creating our platform of platforms.

The platform-of-platforms journey is infinite (it's Pope-Stoop Extenders all the way up). It requires that we always focus first on who we want to help (Strategy No. 1). If we really want to help people, we'll put competition aside, as well as our own immediate goals, and do what's in our customers' best interests. We'll keep rising above our competitors and bring everything and everyone into our embrace.

During the infancy of the New Economy, platforms were mostly about connecting people and companies. Facebook, for example, connected people to people. But now platforms also connect people to machines and machines to other machines.

In the agricultural sector, platforms are emerging around agricultural machines and technology. A company such as John Deere can aggregate beta-level platforms like robotic planting systems, drone-based field-surveillance networks, AI-driven harvesting machines, and remote grain-silo-monitoring equipment. The more integrated and comprehensive the platform, the more attractive it will be to farmers.

We see the growth of platforms in the cryptocurrency and distributed-finance sectors. At first blockchain-based currencies were isolated silos. It was difficult to transfer funds from one cryptocurrency (like bitcoin) to another cryptocurrency (like Ethereum's ether). Then exchanges emerged such as Coinsquare to facilitate trades. Soon we'll see a platform of platforms that will integrate all the exchanges into one master exchange.

We'll see aggregating platforms emerge in artificial intelligence, machine learning algorithms, big data, the IoT, bio-engineering, nanotechnology, 3D printers, and neural networks. These technologies will unite into increasingly higher-level platforms. Even space exploration to the moon, Mars, and beyond will be run on platforms. The space agency with the best, most integrated platform will make it to Mars first.

New factory thinkers view their businesses in terms of platforms, not products and services. The architecture of their companies have four tiers:

Tier 1: Products and Services — They continue to sell products and services such as screwdrivers, potatoes, life insurance, and fitness classes.

Tier 2: Advanced Transformation Programs — They offer their customers "programs" that facilitate a transformation (Strategy No. 14). If they sell mountain bikes, they offer the Mountain Biker Advantage Program. This program provides premium member benefits. They can also elevate their Tier 1 products and services by connecting them to a network such as Wi-Fi-enabled helmets or algorithm-directed route organizers.

Tier 3: Platform — At this level, their businesses make phase transitions into new entities. They no longer simply provide products, services, or programs. They build integrated communities that bring stakeholders together. In the mountain bike example, they connect mountain bikers and link them to other mountain bike companies.

Tier 4: Platform of Platforms — At this tier, they've slipped the surly bonds of competition to reign supreme over all platforms. If other mountain bike platforms appear, they erect a new platform that unites them all. Eternally focused on the evolving needs of their network members, they keep looking for new ways to curate, integrate, and enhance beta resources. At this tier, their businesses are future-proof because they can never be transcended.

Platforms have been around forever. The Catholic Church has been a platform for millennia. Radio and TV networks are platforms. Political parties are platforms. Platforms didn't start with the internet, but they've been empowered by it. As the number of connected people and machines on a network expands and becomes more intertwined, it gets easier to form platforms, even the most specialized and arcane.

The technology part is actually easy. What's harder is adopting a platform mentality. Old ways of thinking, such as a competitive mindset, are hard-wired and deeply rooted in our human psyches. And yet the grandeur of platforms beckons us to realize the next phase in our development. So rise, slip the surly bonds of Earth, and create a platform of platforms.

STRATEGY NO. 16

Speak Metaphorically

My thoughts are stars I cannot fathom into constellations.

— John Green, *The Fault in Our Stars*

I WAS CAUGHT in a vise. I was lost in a deep well of thought. My brain steamed. A week before the big conference in Atlanta, I had chicken feed left in my budget ($100) to pay for the signage in our booth. We had spent a king's ransom on the sponsorship fees plus travel and hotel costs, but we needed to display something in our booth. We couldn't go naked. But what could we do with a pauper's purse? Speaking metaphorically, it was a nightmare.

In the New Economy, we're explorers in an undiscovered country. On this adventure, we continuously encounter alien situations and face novel challenges. To prosper, we must enlist allies by explaining what we've learned quickly and effectively. And the only way to do that in a complex world is to speak metaphorically.

In the old economy, the ability to speak in metaphors, similes, and analogies was primarily the purview of poets. There wasn't a big demand for them on the assembly line. (When I worked in the beer factory, the only metaphors I heard came from the cantankerous foreman who spouted off-colour metaphors that I won't deign to repeat lest I offend my dear readers' delicate sensibilities.)

Today, the ability to work with metaphors is a vital skill. As the world gets more complex, we need to do a better job understanding and explaining what's happening. Otherwise, we could get overwhelmed, freeze up, and be unable to act. We might get swept away on a runaway train with no conductor where the only place of solace is the bar car. (Note: This chapter is a funhouse of metaphors, for both my literary amusement and your instructive edification.)

Metaphors are useful tools for communicating and understanding things that might be hard at first to comprehend. When the internet became mainstream in the 1990s, metaphors were employed to describe it. It was the information highway. It was a web. We surfed it. Metaphors helped people get their heads around the internet, speeding up its adoption.

Metaphors are shorthand. They take something that's well known to explain something that isn't well known. One of my clients used a metaphor to explain financial planning to George Clooney. She was a sponsor at a conference affiliated with the Academy Awards in Los Angeles. The other sponsors gave away products — fur coats, jewellery, electronics, and exotic cars — in the hope that the celebrities would promote them. (When you're rich, people give you things, Tiger Woods once famously said.)

My client got creative and gave out a silver dollar wrapped in bubble wrap. When she gave it to George Clooney, he asked: "What the heck is this?" My client said: "George, you're a famous celebrity, but like all celebrities your money is fragile. One moment you're making millions, the next moment no one wants you in a movie, and you eventually could lose all your money. What I do is help celebrities *bubble wrap* their fragile money."

By using a metaphor (and an object representing the metaphor), she was able to quickly explain the arcane nuances of financial planning to distracted celebrities who were being rushed through a busy conference centre while clutching a swag bag full of free diamond necklaces and ermine ear warmers. And it worked. She got more than six celebrities to become clients from that one event. The organizer of the show told me it was likely the most successful promotion in the event's 20-year history.

There are three tools in this New Economy toolbox — analogies, metaphors, and similes. An analogy compares two things together, for instance, "Having a conversation with my teenager is like trying to get blood from a stone." This analogy explains succinctly that conversing with a sullen teenager is hard, if not impossible.

A metaphor also compares two different things. He is a clown. The car is a lemon. A metaphor is a direct comparison, but the reference has to be discerned. The impression is that the person is foolish and the car doesn't work very well, but the details have to be filled in. This is especially effective in literature because it opens the door to a reader's interpretation. Similes, on the other hand, are more direct by giving more specific details about the comparison. The rain fell like tears. The choir sang like angels.

Turning a complex subject into a catchy analogy isn't as easy as it looks. When I attended the University of Toronto, I wrote 40-page essays on such illuminating topics as "Canada in the Post-Federalist Era" and "Class-Conflict in Europe Following the Black Death." (I'm sure you would love to read those essays.)

I thought I was a pretty good writer until I switched to journalism at Ryerson University. The writing task there was wholly different. We were asked, in five minutes, to take a complex story and boil it down to a single paragraph, then write a short, compelling headline. At first I couldn't do it. I was guilty of "burying" the lead, putting the most interesting and salient facts at the end of the story, not at the beginning. But over time, I got the hang of it. It got easier to recognize the most important news, and in many cases, attach an analogy to the headline: "Campus Crime Spreads Like Virus" or "Student Fees to Skyrocket."

In an economy driven by a connected network, metaphoric communication is like a currency. (See what I did there?) Whether using Twitter, Facebook, or TikTok, it's skillful to utilize metaphors to implant viral ideas. Instead of taking the direct approach, "I don't like," say "His ideas are like a flat pancake" and then add a picture of a pancake. In the first instance, the post will be lost like a pebble in a quarry. But in the second instance, it will shine like a single star in the blackness of space.

Speaking in metaphors is one of our Human Superpowers. Even the most advanced AI has a hard time working with analogies. It doesn't have the unbridled curiosity and embodied pattern recognition needed to construct meaningful analogies and metaphors.

In the dance with robots, we're the poets. Robots do the grunt work so we have the time to think poetically. That's why I believe liberal arts are the best, most utilitarian direction for young, aspiring new factory thinkers. Increasingly, robots will do all the technical work. They'll do the programming. They'll run the mechanics of the world. But we humans will have to make sense of it all and explain our complex world in ways others can comprehend. This requires communication skills — spoken, written, and visual — as well as a facility with analogies and metaphors.

When human beings lived in caves, we survived in a hostile world by telling one another stories, which brought the tribe together as a cohesive unit. The tribe with the best stories won. And now, as robots become both our allies and potential foes, human beings need to recapture their first competitive advantage: storytelling. By using analogies judiciously, we can come together to confront the many challenges we face in the New Economy. Without metaphors, we'll be lost.

And that takes me back the start of this strategy where I faced a dilemma. I had only $100 left for signage on my booth. What to do? I decided to use a metaphor. It was the fastest and cheapest way to solve the problem. I designed a pull-up sign with a picture of a penguin that said: "Do you have the problem with penguins?" That was it, my entire booth, a sign with a penguin on it.

So what happened? At the show, people came up to the booth and asked: "What's the penguin problem?" I told them that most businesses are penguins. They look just like their competitors, so they don't stand out. They're penguins.

The response was excellent. Many people said: "That's us. We're penguins." I told them I could help them package a big idea to stand out from the other penguins in their industries. And they loved it. I got more than a dozen clients from that one show, all with a $100 sign with a metaphor on it.

Be metaphorical. Ask: "What does this situation remind me of?" Come up with an analogy. Be playful. Go ahead, mix metaphors. Light up the metaphorical regions of the mind. It will feel like the dawn after a long, dark night. It will feel like being released from a jail sentence. It will feel like watching colour TV for the first time. (Okay, I'm done. No more metaphors for now. I'm going to put a stopper in it. I'm going to shut the door on analogies.)

STRATEGY NO. 17

Get Paid for Direct Results

I'M A SUCKER for celebrity culture. When I meet a famous person, I find it thrilling. So on one particular night I was tickled to be cheek to jowl with a bevy of sports and media celebrities. A good friend of mine had written a book with a well-known sports icon and invited me to the book launch in appreciation for some consulting I'd done early in the project.

Hobnobbing among the luminaries, my friend introduced me to the publisher of Canada's largest newspaper, someone I'd followed my whole life but had never met. Now in his late seventies, he was one of the few remaining scions of the nation's newspaper industry. My friend introduced him as "the most powerful publisher in the country." To which I replied, somewhat snidely: "Well, power isn't what it used to be, is it?"

Absorbing my somewhat peevish retort, the publishing baron looked down at the floor and said: "What do you mean by that?" At which I launched into a diatribe about the fall of traditional newspaper publishing in the wake of Google, Facebook, and digital media in general. I droned on about how the decline in advertising revenues has decimated old-style newspapers as advertisers flocked to digital media. This migration shifted the power balance from old factory publishers to the owners of digital media companies. Unless newspapers found a new way to generate revenue, I said, stating the obvious, their days were numbered. I ended my screed by saying I actually had some ideas on how to re-engineer the newspaper business model, and if he was interested, I could meet with him to discuss them in more detailed brilliance.

I was feeling a bit cocky that night, so I wasn't actually surprised when the newspaper baron declined my invitation. I'm sure he was just at the party to have a good time and didn't appreciate some guy with a chip on his shoulder pouring salt on his wounds. I wish I'd communicated my message more adroitly, because several months later, news broke that his publishing empire was in dire financial straits and was put up for sale at a bargain price. A once-powerful institution had succumbed to the tidal trends of the New Economy.

Power, indeed, isn't what it used to be. Power has shifted from activity to results. Those in the business of providing an activity suffer in the New Economy. Those in the business of providing results prosper.

Let's start with the poor newspaper publisher. What caused his power to evaporate? In the old-school publishing world, it was all about activity. Newspapers were created through a series of activities: writing articles, selling advertising, designing ads and layouts, printing, and distributing. Lots of activity. All this activity was financed by giving advertisers exposure to its readers in the hope that readers would then buy the advertisers' products.

This business model sustained newspapers for centuries until the New Economy came along and wrecked it. The downfall for newspapers came not just because people increasingly read their news on a screen but because advertisers didn't want to pay for activity anymore. They wanted to pay for results. They were no longer willing to pay for "exposure" in the "hope" that someone would buy something.

Newspapers prospered when they were the only game in town and controlled access to millions of readers. If advertisers wanted to get the word out about their products or services, they had to play a newspaper's game. The newspapers had the power. But, of course, that changed when Google and Facebook came along. Now advertisers could pay them for more direct results — clicks and views. If no one clicked on an ad, nothing was paid. If no one viewed an ad, nothing was paid. But I do say "more" direct results, because this model only took things partway. We're now moving toward a media marketplace based on pure direct results where advertisers only pay a media provider when they make a sale, not just for clicks or views.

If the publishing baron had met with me, I would have laid out this scenario for survival. The newspaper still had tremendous power based on its relationship with its readers, and with its advertisers. But instead of focusing solely on the activity of producing a newspaper, it needed to see its role as a results-driven matchmaker. It could tell its advertisers: "Listen, we have great content and a huge, affluent readership. We can connect you with these readers, and if you make sales, you can compensate us accordingly. If you don't make any sales, you don't have to pay us anything."

This model would save the "newspaper" industry and the profession of journalism. Journalism would be funded by providing companies with direct results, not just exposure and hope that sales might be made for funding a series of activities.

In the New Economy, no one wants to pay for activity. They want to pay for results. This is tough stuff, but it makes economic sense. Ask: "Do you want to pay someone for their activity or for the results they get for you?" The customers of hairstylists, software companies, or farmers aren't really interested in their activities; they're interested in the results they get for them.

Unfortunately, old factory thinking gets in the way. We put a lot of value on the time and effort we put into things. We know all the years we spent in school studying complicated things. We know all the energy we put into creating products or refining services. We know how we've put our hearts and souls into our businesses. But the thing is, the marketplace doesn't want to pay for all that. It wants results. (Don't shoot the messenger here. I think this reality is nasty and brutish, but it is what it is.)

The marketplace has always been predominately results-driven, but it was often difficult to measure direct results. Advertisers got some sense if their advertisements were working but never really knew exactly how well. If we hire a fitness coach, we sense we're feeling more fit but don't know exactly how much healthier we are. If we install a furnace, we might realize some energy efficiency but don't know exactly by how much.

In the New Economy, though, it's much easier to track direct results. Using advanced tracking software, an advertiser can now track exactly how many sales came from each advertisement. Using a fitness tracker, we can see exactly what results we're getting from fitness programs. When we install a new furnace, we can track exactly how much energy, and money, we're saving.

As the network becomes more connected, it will become easier to track results in every area of our lives, and as a result, the incentive will be to only pay for results. So if we run a business, it makes sense to build it around results, not activity, which means constantly viewing things through the perspective of our customers. What results do they seek? How easy is it to track those results? How can we make it possible to achieve better results for our customers, track those results, and then get paid directly for those results?

For example, let's say we have an environmental consulting company. Normally, we get paid to provide advice to clients, say, a water utility. We engage in the activity of giving good advice, and the utility pays us money for that advice. Nice work if we can get it. But in the New Economy, we can provide a higher level of value. For instance, we could install sensors in water treatment plants to track the level of water quality based on certain parameters. Our compensation can then be based on the measurable levels of water quality, not just on our advice or hours of activity.

Measurement is the key reason why this New Economy strategy is so important. The IoT (such as scanners and sensors), the blockchain, machine learning algorithms, and data analytics make it easier to track and measure results. With this exponential growth in measurement tools and capabilities, customers increasingly demand to pay only for results. As such, results-driven competitors emerge to drive out activity-driven incumbents.

Once again, how we think determines how well we adopt this New Economy strategy. Our sadly diminished newspaper baron failed because he couldn't change his way of thinking. He was entranced by the majesty of his operations. He thought his newspaper was about his buildings, equipment, and logistics. He believed it was about paper. He forgot that the whole enterprise rested on whether or not his advertisers actually sold their soap or theatre tickets.

In our dance with robots, we must remember that our customers pay for the dance. They don't care if we do the waltz or the twist with robots; they're only interested in the results they get from the dance.

Going forward, contemplate your customer's situation. What result do they want to achieve? What bigger results can we help them accomplish? How can we help them achieve those bigger results? How can we directly measure those results? What are the metrics and what are the measurement tools? How can we structure our compensation and not base it on activity but on measurable results?

When I contemplate the significance of this New Economy strategy, I envision some interesting scenarios. Take my obsession with celebrities. Perhaps in the near future, I could measure the emotional value I get from celebrities. A device would measure the release of dopamine in my brain's pleasure centre while I watch a movie. As more dopamine is released, a blockchain-enabled system forwards crypto-tokens to the movie producer's account. If no dopamine is released, no tokens are forwarded, and the movie costs me nothing.

Far-fetched? Perhaps. But watch for the emergence of these direct-results business models. Better yet, create them.

STRATEGY NO. 18

Make Problems a Renewable Resource

IN THE MONTH before Covid-19 hit North America, I spent three weeks on a beach in Mexico and a week on the ski slopes of Banff, Alberta. What a time! As I basked in the hot sun and swooshed down the ski runs, I couldn't imagine what lay in store. I now refer to those days of innocence as the "before times." Like all of us, I was oblivious to the havoc about to be unleashed on the world.

When I got home in mid-March 2020, I woke up the next day with dread. The country and the economy were in lockdown. I worried about what would happen to my business. My speaking engagements were being cancelled, and some clients had put their projects on hold. I was scared. But then I remembered Strategy No. 18: Make Problems a Renewable Resource. I realized the world had just offered a whole new crop of problems. I could see opportunity everywhere.

Instead of dread, I felt hopeful and excited. I started thinking about the new problems my customers were now facing. They were stuck at home. Their old economy businesses were threatened. They needed new ideas to survive and even thrive during the pandemic.

Within a day, I created a new venture called the Virtual Business Success Program. I put together a website and promoted a Zoom webinar entitled *How to Create a Virtual Business in 5 Hours*. More than 400 business owners attended the webinar, and we quickly signed up dozens of members in our new program that helped people envision and package new virtual businesses. It was a heady time. My members came to realize that the problems posed by the pandemic were also opportunities in disguise.

Appreciating that problems are opportunities isn't a commonly accepted wisdom in our culture. For the most part, we're a society of complainers. We don't like the problems life puts in our paths. We've been conditioned by consumer culture that life should be a wonderful journey filled with constant pleasures and delights. So when problems come along, we pretend they don't exist or we assume the role of victim. These approaches aren't helpful personally or in our business and professional lives. I've encountered business people who are chronically obsessed with their problems, and their negativity becomes self-fulfilling. By seeing problems as bad, they believe everything is bad.

The key is to see problems as a renewable resource. Every time a problem is solved, it tends to procreate a progeny of new problems. We can then prosper by seeking solutions to these new problems, which sire even more new problems/opportunities.

It's all about attitude and perspective. First, we need to see problems in a more positive light — that new problems give us the opportunity to help people in new ways. And secondly, by assuming the perspective of the customer, we realize that focusing on solving the problems of others is better than ruminating on our own problems. Furthermore, we realize that solving other people's problems is often the best way to solve many of our own.

Let's imagine what would happen if everyone woke up tomorrow determined to help other people solve their problems. My bet is that the economy would skyrocket. Millions of jobs would be created. Many mental health issues would disappear. People would be happier.

In the old economy, working on the assembly line was a task to keep production moving. We weren't asked to think about other people's problems, only to keep our heads down, stay on task, not look up, not look around, remain focused, and keep the line moving.

But in the New Economy, our tasks are different. Using unbridled curiosity, we look around and ask questions. What's going on? What's changed? What do people need today that they didn't need yesterday? What are the trend lines? Where are things headed?

Then we can use our powers of embodied pattern recognition to discern the bigger picture. What new problems are emerging? What are the underlying causes of these problems?

These reflections lead to our human talent for purpose-driven ideation. What are possible solutions to these problems? How can we combine existing resources into new combinations to solve these problems? What new technology, strategies, and processes are needed?

Each of these Human Superpowers are supported by ethical framing. How can we solve these problems in the most ethical way possible? How can we minimize the negative impact created by solving these problems? How can we minimize harm and maximize well-being?

Finally, we can use metaphoric communication to adroitly explain the new problem, its negative repercussions, and new creative solutions. Using analogies and creative stories, we marshal resources faster, get people on board more expeditiously, and solve the problems faster.

In the dance with robots, we'll create a steady supply of problems. As technology becomes more advanced and the complexity of the network grows, billions of new problems will emerge. These conundrums shouldn't come as a surprise; they should be expected. Looking forward, we can't know exactly what problems will emerge, but we can be certain that new problems are inevitable.

Don't let anyone try to convince you otherwise.

Take cryptocurrencies. When bitcoin and other blockchain-based currencies were introduced, they were heralded as a safe way to hold and exchange value. Transactions recorded in an immutable distributed ledger would be safer and more egalitarian than fiat currencies controlled by central banks and large financial institutions. What could go wrong?

In 2018, hackers broke into Coincheck, a cryptocurrency exchange, and made off with more than $350 million. In 2018, hackers absconded with more than $730 million in funds. In 2013 and 2014, online robbers fleeced the Mt. Gox crypto-exchange out of 850,000 bitcoins. In 2021, some people lost millions because they couldn't remember the passwords to their crypto-currency wallets.

Consider identity theft, a problem that exploded when our personal information got stored online. Studies show that 1 in 15 Americans have had their identities stolen. More than 1 in 4 adults, age 55 and over, have had their identities pilfered.

Expanding internet connectivity has led to the rise of extremism and societal discord. Social media shaming has increased the rates of teenage suicide. New Economy business models have wiped out old economy companies. Millions of people have lost their jobs due to automation.

This is just a small selection of the problems spawned by technology in the New Economy. But instead of getting depressed about it, the path forward is to become problem solvers.

As we adopt these New Economy strategies in a fulsome manner and push through our old factory mental blocks, we come to see a startling truth: we've only created about 1 percent of the value that can and will be created. The Industrial Revolution was a good start, but the New Economy is going to be so much bigger and better. A decade from now we'll do things we can't imagine today. We'll solve problems that don't exist right now.

The most constant feature of the universe is change. Change creates problems. Constant change makes problems a renewable resource. Our New Economy job is to make the most of this renewable resource.

STRATEGY NO. 19

Combine Digital with Analogue

AS HE PUT the toy truck down on the desk, Doug felt a tad foolish. He wondered what his prospect — the billionaire owner of the country's biggest construction company — would think about his silly marketing stunt.

"What's this?" the billionaire asked, eagerly picking up the truck.

"The truck represents your life, your future," Doug said. "Do you know where your truck is headed?"

Pausing for a second, deep in thought, the billionaire replied, "You know, I haven't got a clue where my truck is headed."

"Well, that's what I do," Doug explained. "I'll help you get your truck pointed in the right direction."

The next day, Doug told me what happened next.

"We had an awesome chat. He shared things with me he's never told anyone before. It was remarkable. He loved the toy truck. He kept picking it up and playing with it. Like a little kid. And the best part? He signed up for my program on the spot. He wrote me a cheque for $25,000. And I think it was all because of that toy truck. It was very meaningful to him. So it was a big success, but frankly I'm still surprised it worked."

Doug was surprised the toy truck gambit worked because he was still waking up from the digital dream. When I met Doug, he had built his business plan around digital. His dream was: "I'll send out emails and post things to social media, and the prospects will come flocking to me. And then I'll meet them on Zoom and they'll pay me with a digital transfer. I'll never have to meet anyone."

Like many dreams, Doug's digital dream turned into a nightmare. His emails and social media posts didn't work. Prospects didn't respond. He scored only a few Zoom meetings with prospects. His closing rate was terrible. By taking the human element out of his work, his business was tanking.

I told Doug his plight was common. Many of us buy into the idea that everything should be done digitally. Vendors of digital tools tell us that analogue is old school and should be replaced. They peddle Technopia, a fundamentalist view that all new technology is good and better than the old. But I've learned that the better approach is to adopt Strategy No. 19: Combine Digital with Analogue.

This strategy is seminal to the premise of this book. Success in the New Economy is the skillful combining of the digital (robots) with the analogue (humans).

While digital technology can be extremely powerful, it can only offer a representation of reality. When we digitize something, like a song recording, we lose something in the translation. As biological beings we have a deep attachment to the analogue because we're analogue. That's why vinyl record sales are booming. Even though we can get every song in the world streamed to our smartphones for pennies a day, people have rediscovered the joy of listening to a vinyl record on a turntable. They enjoy the fuller, richer sound of vinyl. They like the physical nature of the experience. They'll also pay $20 or more (sometimes a lot more) for a vinyl record, even though they can listen to the same song on their phone.

In the New Economy, look for a resurgence of analogue. As we become more enmeshed in a robot world, humans will seek respite in analogue. Analogue products and services will be coveted more than ever, sometimes in surprising ways.

Think about an in-person meeting. During the pandemic, we were forced to meet on Zoom and other teleconferencing sites, but the trend toward video conferencing was already under way long before Covid-19. Digital meetings are faster, easier, and cheaper. But, of course, a digital meeting is just a replica of an in-person meeting. Most of us would rather have a real meeting if we could, which in a world of robots makes a real meeting relatively more valuable. It feels like a premium experience. I noticed this phenomenon in my work building The New Economy Network. When possible, my goal was to meet with my members individually, in person, usually for a coffee at Starbucks. I started to notice that the quality of the relationships I built with people at Starbucks far surpassed those that were only through video conferencing. I did more business and got more opportunities from my analogue relationships. I could tell that the folks I met in person felt special, more valued.

In the digital realm, things are devalued by ubiquity. When you can access a billion songs instantly, no song is special. Every song is a commodity. But when we have to pull a vinyl record out of an album jacket and then place it on a turntable, a song takes on a more rarefied premium quality. It's not just that the song sounds better on vinyl; it's that the vinyl song requires time and effort and is more difficult to consume. This gives the vinyl song more meaning.

It's a misconception to think that disruptive technology always replaces its predecessors. It's more common for new technology or business models to provide another option. Consider television. It didn't replace radio. Some people prefer radio to TV. Or they listen to radio in the morning as they get ready for work and then watch TV in the evening.

When it comes to digital, beware the digital dream. It might not be the best move to replace everything analogue. A hybrid strategy might be a better way to go. For example, if we rely solely on digital marketing, we might consider sending our prospects something analogue through the mail, like a hand-painted card.

Imagine what would happen. Our prospects probably get dozens of email solicitations every day and likely ignore most of them. But then they get a hand-painted card. They're not going to ignore it. They don't get one of those every day. It's special. Going analogue helps us stand out and raises the chance that our prospects might take a meeting with us.

You could also combine digital and analogue. You could send out the hand-painted card and then send an email asking prospects if they got it. Then a meeting could be requested, either by video conference or in person. We could insist on in-person meetings. We could tell our prospects they'll get much more value out of them.

When it comes to products and services, don't think everything needs to be virtual or digital in the New Economy. If our competitors all go digital, we might tack back toward analogue. We might create a board game rather than a VR video game. We might publish a super-size printed book that isn't available digitally. We might open a pop-up retail store or sell retro items like slide rules or typewriters. The key is to keep our minds open and not neglect the potential of analogue.

This strategy has been fruitful for my clients with online courses. At first their digital dream was that thousands of people would buy their online courses and the money would roll in. But they soon realized the market was flooded with online courses, many of them free. No matter how little they charged, it was hard to compete with free. So we suggested adding a human element so that their courses would now include live interaction with trainers or coaches. Using this hybrid model, my clients can charge hundreds, even thousands, of dollars for their courses. By adding the analogue (human), it makes their courses more attractive to buyers.

We can also add digital to something analogue. If we have a tangible product like a bike, we can add a digital component to it. That's what Peloton did. It attached online classes to its spin bike, allowing its "members" to interact with one another and monitor their progress in real time. Like Peloton, anything analogue can benefit from being connected digitally to the network. Whatever the object is, its value can increase exponentially when it becomes a connected object.

Amazon represents another manifestation of this New Economy strategy. The company has mastered digital, robot-driven logistics to deliver tangible products quickly and cheaply — analogue things. It beat out its competition because it has a better system for moving analogue things around. That's why I keep buying from Amazon. I'd love to spread my largesse by buying from other companies, but those firms typically have inferior distribution and delivery systems. I'd rather get my package today than wait 10 days.

Until robots start buying stuff, we have to keep reminding ourselves that our customers are analogue beings. They don't want their whole lives to be digital. They still crave connecting with people in the "bio-verse." They want to hold things in their hands. They want to smell things, taste things, and feel things. They want real-life experiences.

In the New Economy, people will pay good money for analogue. A lot of money. People pay $300 for a limited-edition vinyl record or $50,000 for handmade designer luggage.

In the New Economy, the marketplace has bifurcated into two distinct camps: fast food and gourmet. On the fast-food side, we have anything that's perceived as a commodity, mostly things that are digital. On the gourmet side, we have anything that's considered to be special and premium, mostly things that are analogue. On the fast-food side, the best price is free, so anything sold in this market must compete on price against free alternatives. On the premium side, higher prices mean the product or service is even more special.

That's why analogue is a huge opportunity in the New Economy. While everyone rushes into digital, nurture the analogue side.

Consider financial services. Online financial services (known as robo-advisers) are popular because of their lower management fees. Human financial advisers who charge 1 to 2 percent can't compete against robo-advisers that charge .5 percent or less (sometimes even nothing). The only way for human advisers to compete with robot advisers is to fully exploit their human analogue capabilities and to charge premium prices. That's why I coach financial service clients to create premium programs that go well beyond what their customers can get from a robo-adviser. It's no longer viable for human advisers to sell their investment portfolio skills when an algorithm can do the same job faster, better, and for much less money. Instead, human advisers need to sell their wisdom, relationship skills, listening and communication skills, and ability to see and integrate the big picture. They need to market their Human Superpowers.

Robots will win the digital game because they're digital. We can win the analogue game because we're analogue. So we must look at what we can do in the analogue realm that transcends what's available in the digital realm. That's why I keep pointing back to our Five Human Superpowers: embodied pattern recognition, unbridled curiosity, purpose-driven ideation, ethical framing, and metaphoric communication. These Human Superpowers are analogue, and by marketing them, we can add tremendous value in the New Economy.

That's what my client Doug did. When he gave the toy truck to the billionaire, he used this New Economy strategy to great effect. The tactile nature of the truck captured the imagination of the prospect. It was meaningful to him. The fact that Doug was present in his office and not just in a video conference made the prospect see Doug, and himself, as special. What's more, Doug's coaching program was deliciously analogue. By getting to know his client on a deep, personal level, Doug used embodied pattern recognition and unbridled curiosity to discern his client's emotional condition. He employed purpose-driven ideation and ethical framing to develop solutions to the client's problems, while utilizing metaphoric communication to explain these new strategies in a way that was easily understood. Of course, the toy truck itself was a perfect example of metaphoric communication.

So don't ignore analogue in a fever of robot-mania. Remember that a hybrid sensibility — the artful dance of the digital and the analogue, the robot and the human — offers much greater opportunities for success in the New Economy.

STRATEGY NO. 20

Invent the Future

IN THE OPENING act of William Shakespeare's *Macbeth*, three witches tell Macbeth that one day he'll be king of Scotland. They add the cryptic prophecy that his friend Banquo's children will also be kings. With these quixotic predictions in his mind, Macbeth embarks on a path of murder and mayhem. He kills Banquo, who then haunts him relentlessly, then murders a host of other men, women, and children. He does indeed become king, but as in all good Shakespearean tragedies, he meets his demise in the final act.

Like the witches in Macbeth, robots predict the future. They use machine learning algorithms and big sets of data to make predictions. They predict the best routes to take home and give accurate ETAs. They predict what we might want to say in texts or emails and give us suggestions. They predict what the stock market might do tomorrow or what products we might want to buy from Amazon. Prediction is one of a robot's most important functions.

Robots can predict the future, but they can't invent it. Their predictions are rooted in the present and past. They look at what's happening now and what happened in the past, then project it into the future. This past-present-future process can be extremely helpful, but it's not particularly creative or inventive. It doesn't leave much room for radical ideas or paradigm shifts. If robots had been around in 1890, they might have predicted that we wanted faster horses. They wouldn't have predicted or invented the car. It's not in their DNA to make such creative leaps.

But more concerning is that robot predictions can be self-fulfilling. Like the witches' prophecies, the predictions of robots can cause a lot of toil and trouble. Blindly following them can lead to undesirable outcomes, even tragedy. Two crashes of the Boeing 737 MAX 8, which killed hundreds of people, were caused by an onboard software system that predicted the wrong things due to a faulty sensor. Given erroneous information, the pilots and the automated flight control system were caught in a futile struggle that forced the planes into nosedives.

The moral of *Macbeth* is that by following the witches' prophecies the protagonist set off on a path to make them come true. The question is: Would Macbeth have pursued that same path if the witches hadn't put the idea — becoming king — in his head? It's unlikely. He would have probably remained a loyal subject of the Scottish realm and lived a relatively prosperous and uneventful life. Instead of following a prediction, he would have invented his own future.

As robots become more powerful, their predictive capacity grows exponentially. And these predictions morph from suggestions to subtle commands. They tell us what our future should be and what future we should make true. Take this route to work. Wear a hat. Go to this island for a holiday. Marry this person and live in that house. Drive this kind of car and send the kids to that school.

Prediction robots are hard to resist. Their predictions (suggestions) make a lot of sense. Their predictions give our lives direction and certainty. They make us feel empowered, in command. But that's a delusion. Macbeth thought he charted his own destiny but was manipulated by the witches. They ran his life, not him.

The ultimate danger of prediction robots is that they hand us a future on a platter that won't be the future we actually want or could have. That's why it's important to follow Strategy No. 20: Invent the Future.

In the New Economy, we can get overwhelmed by the rush of changing events and the endless flashbang of news, ideas, and opinions. We can get swept away. But if we spend time to contemplate our future and invent it, we can take back control.

A few years ago, I gave a workshop for a group of business owners in western Canada. The conclave was hosted by the owner of a taxi company. During my talk, I innocently mentioned Uber as an example of a disruptive New Economy business. At that, the taxi guy shot up out of his chair and launched into a 10-minute rant about how much he hated Uber. The digital upstart had cut deeply into his business and forced down the value of his company.

I understood his frustration but knew he was actually mad about something else. It wasn't just because Uber had screwed up his business. He was mad because he didn't think up the idea himself and had missed the boat.

The question is: Why didn't the taxi guy think up Uber? After all, he's in the industry. Wasn't he in the best position to invent a new kind of taxi system?

The answer is sadly typical. The taxi guy didn't invent Uber because he never spent a second to think about the future. He focused solely on the present. Every day he worked hard on his business, upgrading his accounting software and changing the colour of the taxis. But the improvements were incremental. They would never lead to an idea like Uber. In fact, by focusing solely on improving his existing business, he was even less likely to invent a new future.

Remember, we human beings have the *status quo bias*. We tend to assume the future will be more or less the same as the present — perhaps with faster computers, better iPhones, and a few robots running around — but generally the same. We don't spend much time imagining completely different scenarios for the future.

In Toronto, where I live, the local politicians have committed to building an extension of the subway system. The project will add only three stations, cost billions of dollars, and won't be ready for a decade. Now, I'm a big supporter of public transit, but it would have been a good idea for City Council to spend a little bit of time, even an hour, to ponder other future scenarios. Perhaps people won't take subways 10 years from now. Maybe a network of autonomous vehicles will replace them. Instead of taking a subway, a robot on wheels or a drone will pick up people at their homes and drop them off at their exact destinations. Maybe the trip will be paid for by cryptocurrency.

I don't know if that will happen, or could happen, but it's worth considering how the future might be different before we invest billions of dollars in an infrastructure project.

So take a different approach. Spend time and energy thinking about the future. Take what's been learned in this book and come up with new ideas for the future. Ask: "How will our future be new, better, and different from the present? How will we use these New Economy strategies to invent the future we want? How will we take advantage of all the new tools and technology available?"

There's one simple technique that makes future-crafting much easier. To begin, put everything currently done into a box (figuratively). Call this box old factory. It's an old factory because it represents the past. That doesn't mean there's anything wrong with the old factory; just put it aside for now. We don't try to change it or transform it. If we do that, we might end up with faster horses or taxis of a different colour.

With the old factory tucked away, we turn our attention to the new one. In a sense, we go across the street to a vacant lot where we can build a new structure from scratch with all new parts. We're completely liberated to invent a totally new and better future.

So what will our new factory future look like? I suggest starting with this book's first strategy: Achieve Well-Being Using Fewer Resources. Then ask: "What can we do in the future that will enable us and others to experience greater well-being while employing less time, money, and energy?"

Next, move on to Strategy No. 2: Focus First on Who We Want to Help. Make the future about other people, not something personal. Ask: "Who do we really want to work with? Who can benefit most from our ideas and goodwill? Where can we find more of these ideal people?"

The third pillar for a new future can be constructed with Strategy No. 3: Build a Value Proposition Around a Big Idea. Ask: "What big problem can we help our customers solve, a problem no one else is helping them with? What big goals can we help them achieve?

Remember here to think big and start small (Strategy No. 13). When we invent the future, we'll be more motivated if the vision is huge.

Be forewarned that inventing the future isn't easy. Some people will scoff at our future visions. They'll try to thwart us. Be careful who those visions are shared with. (My shop teacher in high school said: "Never show a fool a job half done.")

Remember, we don't have to get anyone's permission or validation to invent the future.

I've confronted naysayers my whole life. When I was 25, I started an entertainment newspaper called *The Uptown Magazine*. I was determined to invent this new future, and I thought everyone would be supportive. They weren't. Some friends and family were skeptical. "That's a pretty big undertaking for a young person," someone said. "The marketplace doesn't need another magazine," another quipped. "You'll go broke," someone predicted.

But I never listen to people who conflate negativity with wisdom. I was hell-bent to invent the future. And it worked. The magazine was profitable starting with the first issue, something unheard of in the publishing industry. It was a popular success and led to the formation of my publishing and marketing company.

Most importantly, it taught me how to invent the future. Since those early days, inventing the future has been a key habit in our company. Every quarter we spend a full day to think about the future. We ask one fundamental question: "What do we want the future to be?"

This strategy is very important in the New Economy because robots set their own trajectory for the future. Like the witches in *Macbeth*, they offer us a suggested future on a platter like a free sample of cheese at the supermarket. It's enticing. But it might not be the cheese we really want to eat.

The best way to predict the future is to invent it.

STRATEGY NO. 21

Hold the Centre

Things fall apart; the centre cannot hold;
Mere anarchy is loosed upon the world ...

— William Butler Yeats, "The Second Coming"

IN THE 1990S when the internet and the World Wide Web went main-stream, pundits predicted the demise of hierarchy and the end of the middle-man. People could now produce their own websites, personally broadcast podcasts and videos, and participate in open discussions no longer mediated by elite politicians, media companies, and other power brokers. They could also sell their products and services directly to customers without going through distributors and retailers. Dictators would fall. It was the end of hierarchy. The world was flat.

Of course, that's not what happened. New forms of hierarchy arose to re-place the old hierarchy. Companies such as Google, Facebook, Amazon, and Apple became the overlords of the digital era. Vendors on these platforms were forced to pay high commissions to sell their products. Social media sites like Facebook dominated the media landscape and dictators figured out how to exploit the internet as a tool for social control. Rather than creating a more egalitarian economy and society, inequality worsened. Most of the benefits and power of the internet boom accrued to the 1 percent, more precisely to the 1 percent of the 1 percent. As The Who lament in their song "Won't Get Fooled Again": "Meet the new boss / Same as the old boss."

And yet there's now a counter-movement to bring down these neo-hierarchies and redistribute wealth and power back to the masses. Primarily driven by blockchain technology, this movement aims once again to eliminate the middle person (I use a genderless noun here, but most middle persons are still middlemen).

The promise of the blockchain has yet to be realized as I write this book, but it's more useful as a philosophy than as a technology. A blockchain is a ledger of transactions that is "distributed." For example, the cryptocurrency bitcoin runs on a blockchain. Every time two people exchange bitcoins, the bitcoin ledger is updated to record that transaction. All the transactions ever made with bitcoins are stored on the ledger. But here's the key point. This ledger isn't held by just one person or organization, it's held by thousands of parties. When there's a bitcoin transaction, all the ledgers are updated. Most important to understanding the philosophy of the blockchain, there's no central organization controlling the ledger. In essence, there's no centre.

That's why the blockchain is more than just a useful technology. If and when it comes into full fruition as a means of production in our economy, it will bring a tsunami of change in its wake. Imagine a world where transactions are carried out using a distributed rather than centralized system. Banks would be obsolete. Instead of a bank controlling the ledger (and holding our money in a vault), we'd all have a copy of the ledger (and hold our money in our crypto-wallet). One attraction of this distributed model is that we would no longer pay fees to a bank.

A decentralized distributed economy will affect every industry. Collectively, we could provide insurance to one another. No more insurance companies. We could create our own ride-sharing system. No more Uber or Lyft. We could create our own audio and video selling system. No more Netflix or Spotify. In each case, the collective users of these systems would control how they operate and no longer pay fees to the owner of the system.

Already, there are many applications of decentralized systems, some of them quite innovative. Based on an early tip from my son-in-law, I was one of the first participants in a blockchain game called CryptoKitties. In this game, you collect and breed virtual cats. You earn cryptocurrency by buying and selling your cats, putting them out to sire with other cats. It's entertaining, but it can also be lucrative. One CryptoKitty sold for more than US$100,000. Crazy, right? I said I was fortunate to get in early because my CryptoKitties are quite valuable; they're 10th generation or earlier. They have desirable virtual DNA, so people pay me to breed their cats with mine. My CryptoKitties spread their DNA during amorous encounters, and I make money. What a world!

If it seems as if I've gone off the deep end, that might be right. When I started playing CryptoKitties, I was disoriented. I thought: *What the heck is this?* I found it strange that there was no single organization that owned CryptoKitties. It was managed by a collective group of participants who had played God by bringing the first CryptoKitties into the world and then set them free to go forth and multiply. It was also apparent that this blockchain game had an underlying value proposition that combined entertainment and a financial incentive. I could make money while having fun.

Distributed systems will disrupt hundreds of industries in the next decade: real estate, education, retail, health care, supply-chain management, energy, entertainment, sports, the non-profit sector, law, publishing, resource management, agriculture, travel, waste management, and accounting. If we're in one of those industries, we need to look more closely at how the blockchain and other decentralized systems will affect the future. Market forces make this trend inevitable for two reasons: one financial, one societal.

Financially, there's a monetary incentive to decentralize. Currently, the entities that control central systems charge high fees to facilitate transactions. For example, Netflix charges fees to both movie companies and viewers. If a new decentralized system comes along that doesn't charge fees, or charges much lower ones, people will have a financial incentive to switch.

From a societal perspective, humans strive to be free. They don't generally like to be controlled or under the thumb of an overlord. They resent it. So when they're given the choice to participate in a decentralized system with no overlord, they jump at the chance. That's one reason why cryptocurrencies are popular. It's not just the potential to make money that attracts people. Owning cryptocurrencies makes us feel free. No more banks and government control. Power to the people!

This trend gains traction as decentralization and the sharing economy converge. A distributed energy system, for example, has no centralized energy production utility. Users in the system produce their own energy, such as solar and wind, and then share their excesses on the network, making them "prosumers" who act simultaneously as consumers and producers.

The distributed sharing of computer processing will also occur. Just in the same way that a spare bedroom can be rented to people on Airbnb, the idle processing capacity of a personal computer or iPhone can also be rented out. A blockchain could keep track of the people using our processors and compensate us for these micro-transactions. Money can be made while we and our computers sleep.

Decentralization driven by the blockchain revives the original egalitarian vision of the internet. Back in the 1980s and 1990s, we didn't really know what we were getting into. HTML and the World Wide Web were incredible tools, but the internet wasn't designed based on some grand plan. That's why the internet has been plagued by privacy issues, hacking, threats to democracy, and the exacerbation of inequality. Perhaps now we can create a better internet.

So how do we prosper in a decentralized New Economy? How do we manage in systems with no leader, no hierarchy, no central authority? The way forward is to employ Strategy No. 21: Hold the Centre.

As these decentralized systems and models take hold and eclipse their centralized ancestors, hold together both polarities. The mistake is to think there are only two choices: centralized or decentralized. The smart approach is to combine them.

Consider the idea that the blockchain might replace banks. I don't think that's going to occur, at least it doesn't need to happen. While the blockchain might take over banking's ledger function, people will still need help to manage their money. Bankers will become advisers rather than protectors of a vault.

Let's say that a new co-operative system replaces Uber or Lyft. Consumers negotiate directly with drivers for a trip downtown. No middle person. But what if there's a quality issue? What if there's a complaint? Who gets called? Who rectifies the situation? Perhaps that could be us. We could put ourselves forward as the customer-service arm of the network. Users would pay us to investigate the problem and deal with the driver in question. Or perhaps we could put ourselves forward to recruit new drivers. Drivers would pay us a fee for training and onboarding.

This is an exciting opportunity. In the old centralized economy, we seek employment from a centralized authority. It gives us full-time or contract work. It can also fire us. But in the decentralized economy, we make our own deals. We put ourselves forward to the network and present our value propositions. If people want to use our services, they pay us directly. In a customer-service scenario, it's like the customer who pays a clerk at a store directly rather than the employer. We'll all be employers and employees for one another in a giant network.

Note that this isn't the gig economy. Personally, I love the gig economy, but I know others have problems with it. I understand their concerns. I don't want people to be exploited. But in a distributed economy, we have greater agency. No central power has the ability to exploit or coerce anyone. We're compensated for the true values we bring to the network and our roles in it.

Even in a distributed system, leadership is important. The people who pioneered bitcoin and CryptoKitties have done well for themselves. They came up with a big idea, put it together, and launched it. As the founding members, they don't own equity in the traditional sense, but they have a lot of influence and power. They've also made a lot of money.

So don't think that the distributed nature of the New Economy is some kind of Bolshevik revanchism. It's capitalism in a purer, more egalitarian form. It gives power to the people by creating more value and distributes more evenly the rights, responsibilities, and rewards of the system.

It also makes the economy more efficient. For example, consider this scenario. Someone speeds down the highway in her autonomous rover-pod while watching a movie on Hot Popcorn, the blockchain movie network. She receives a text message: "Would you like to earn 1,000 accelerator tokens by slowing down your ride? One of our members is in a hurry to get downtown and would like to pass you."

Given that she wants to finish the movie before she gets to her destination, she thinks it's a good idea, so she hits the okay button. Immediately, her rover-pod decelerates and moves into the slow lane. To her left, she sees a red rover-pod streak by as 1,000 accelerator tokens are deposited in her crypto-wallet. She just made money for slowing down and taking it easy. What a way to make a living!

Usually, when I talk about these scenarios, people think I just ate some bat dung. But watch out for the *status quo bias*. The future is going to be a lot different. The traditional centralized structures that held our society together are dissolving. It sounds scary, but it's not necessarily a bad thing. If we hold the centre in a decentralized world, we'll prosper. We'll also provide the leadership that's needed.

STRATEGY NO. 22

Pay Attention

IT WAS THE store opening seen around the world. In 1992, my client Granada TV wanted publicity for the opening of its new flagship store on Yonge Street in downtown Toronto. While I always welcomed a marketing challenge, I knew it would be tough to get the media interested in the launch of a small retail store. It wasn't much of a story. But I got to work. I invited the media to a grand-opening party. I arranged a fireworks display and hired a photographer to take pictures. I invited TV celebrities to attend. But try as I might, only a handful of reporters agreed to show up. It was shaping up to be a public relations disaster.

But sometimes you make your own luck. On the evening of the store opening, the Toronto Blue Jays won the American League championship series against the Oakland Athletics. It was the first time that a non-U.S. team won a pennant in Major League Baseball history. Torontonians were ecstatic, and following the win, more than a million people took to the streets, specifically Yonge Street, right in front of the Granada TV store.

Sensing an opportunity, I told my photographer to get on the roof of the building across the street so he could get a picture of the crowd surrounding the store. Then I got a huge break. I spotted the film crew from CNN and told them I was just about to set off a huge fireworks display. I suggested they join my photographer at the top of the building for the perfect shot.

Guess what happened. CNN captured video of the massive crowd on Yonge Street as it cheered the fireworks blazing from atop the Granada TV store. The video was subsequently aired dozens of times on CNN and was picked up by other networks around the world. It was estimated that more than 200 million people saw the footage, which prominently displayed Granada TV and its new store. Talk about a home run!

Like Granada TV, everyone in business wants attention. We want customers to take notice of us. To think about us. To keep thinking about us. And then to buy from us.

Marketing is all about attention. The more attention we get, the more potential business we get. In the old economy, we usually sought attention through traditional media like newspapers, magazines, radio, and television. My job as a PR agent was to get my clients featured in the media by proposing story ideas to editors and producers. Something catchy but also credible. An editor or producer acted as curator and gatekeeper. They carefully selected the stories that appeared in the media. They decided who got attention and who didn't.

But in the New Economy, there are no gatekeepers. On the network, everyone competes for attention. Generally speaking, the crazier the content, the more attention it gets. Even if we don't want to, when someone posts an outrageous comment or video, we pay attention, even if the content and its purveyor disgust us. It's like slowing down to look at a car wreck. We can't help ourselves. As we've seen, this desire to get attention, coupled with the ability to broadcast whatever we want to potentially billions of people at virtually no cost, fuels demagoguery, extremism, discord, conspiracy theories, and a degradation of civil discourse. Sadly, the voices of reason and civility get drowned out by the shrill bleating of opportunists.

Robots have made the situation worse. Social media and vendor platforms are powered by algorithms to garner attention, to keep us engaged so we don't wander off and do something else. Alerts, notifications, and pop-ups are designed to grab our attention just as it might be diverted elsewhere.

Think of these algorithms as robots that keep saying: "Look here, look here. Pay attention here, pay attention here."

As humans, we only have so much attention to give. It's a finite resource. Although we might think we can multi-task our way through life, we can actually only pay attention to one thing at a time. And there are only so many hours and minutes in our waking days. That's why attention-seekers are so desperate. They know we can only pay attention to a few things out of the multitude of options. That's why they ramp up their attention tactics. They'll do anything to keep us focused on them. That's why they constantly track what we're doing online. They use robots to find out what we pay attention to so they can feed us more of the same to keep us paying attention. It's an endless loop.

Of course, we're not innocent in this war of attention. We choose to spend hours doom-scrolling through Twitter or crave-scrolling on Amazon or Alibaba. We lose weeks binge-watching on Netflix or selfie-surfing on Facebook. And at the end of the day, we wonder what it was all about and feel as if we just ate a giant bag of digital potato chips. It's a form of attentional bankruptcy.

In the New Economy, we must pay attention to what we pay attention to. We must see our attention capacity as a limited and valuable asset that's not to be squandered. We must invest our attention in what's worthy of our attention, what nurtures us, and what fosters the common good. Of course, we'll often get distracted by a shiny object. But we can protect ourselves by understanding the source of the shiny object: who made it and what are they really up to (they want your attention)? By cultivating this kind of literacy, we can manage our attention resources more wisely. We can turn our attention deficit into an attention surplus.

From a business perspective, we must learn to be good practitioners in the attention marketplace. Certainly, we want to get attention for our businesses, and we should. But we must do it respectfully. We must also be clear about our intentions.

That's why my coaching company focuses on big ideas. Big ideas are something new, better, and different that our customers can only get from us. They're one of a kind. Exceptional. When we communicate a big idea, it gets attention because our audiences have never heard about such a thing before. That's why I talk about lobsters and penguins and basketballs — and robots — because they get attention. They're also memorable.

It's also important that our big idea be credible. It must be based on an intention to be helpful. As people become more savvy in the New Economy, they get better at calling out malignant attention-seekers. They see what such people are doing — putting out crazy, hateful content to get attention. Sure, many folks are still fooled by these con artists, but they're probably not their customers. Their customers are likely more discerning. So if we try to play the shiny object game by putting out noxious vapourware — meaning there's nothing real inside — it won't work and will likely backfire. If we take the wrong tack, the network will turn on us in an instant.

So toe a fine balance. Respectfully ask for attention. Give people a good, wholesome reason to pay attention. Keep their attention by moderating how often we ask for it. Don't overdo it and don't underdo it. Also remember that we need to play the attention game. Don't drop out altogether. If we don't get the attention of our customers, our competitors will.

Ultimately, we're what we pay attention to. If we pay attention to things that are hateful, we become hateful. If we pay attention to things that foster greed, we become greedy. If we pay attention to lies, we become liars.

Thankfully, the reverse is true. If we pay attention to what's loving, we become loving. If we pay attention to what's generous, we become generous. If we pay attention to what's true, we become truthful.

So pay attention to what you pay attention to.

STRATEGY NO. 23

Be an Industry Outsider

IN THE NEW Economy, the idea of "industries" is obsolete. It's a relic from the old economy where everyone was supposed to know their places, stay in their lanes, and not rock the boat. In a fast-changing marketplace run on a network, our customers don't care what industry we think we belong to. They just want us to provide them with value. That's why Strategy No. 23 is Be an Industry Outsider.

The idea that we're part of an industry is a mental trap. We think: *This is what a company in this industry does, and this is what it doesn't do.* These self-imposed restrictions are reinforced by the bureaucracy of the industry — associations, regulatory organizations, governments — and anyone who makes a living by maintaining the viability of an industry.

In the New Economy, industries are irrelevant. As I said, our customers don't care what industry we belong to. They don't care if we have a long line of designations after our names and a wall full of diplomas or certifications from industry educational institutions. They just want us to provide them with value. But unfortunately, by shackling our minds to the boundaries of an industry, it's hard to develop new kinds of value. At best, we can come up with incremental improvements, but we're unlikely to invent anything truly different or groundbreaking.

That's why we need to throw out the idea of industries. Ask: "What industry is Apple in? What industry is Google in? What industry is Amazon in?" When I ask people these questions, they try to fit these companies into boxes. Perhaps Apple is a consumer electronics company. Okay, but what about the fact that it also sells music, movies, and apps? Do those fit in the electronics category? Well, no, but ...

You see, it's irrelevant what industry Apple is in. It isn't in any industry. If the term has to be used, Apple is in the Apple industry. It can do whatever it wants. The universe is its oyster. That's why it's one of the biggest companies in the world; it's an industry outsider.

The same goes for Google and Amazon. We can't put them into any kind of category or industry. This also applies to LEGO, Harley-Davidson, Facebook, and Peloton. They don't belong in any industry. They're their own industries.

Of course, we all start out in an industry. I began in the communications industry. I earned a bachelor of arts in journalism and started a community newspaper, which led to the creation of my publishing company. Then I started an internet service provider (ISP) and built bulletin board service (BBS) networks. After that I created a digital marketing consulting division and a website design department, then launched an innovation packaging program. Each of these new services was layered on top of the others. Generally speaking, my company and I could be placed in the marketing and publishing industries, but I don't think of it that way. My company is in the business of helping our customers in whatever way we can.

That's why I don't spend a lot of time attending industry trade shows or trying to win industry awards. Rather, I go to trade shows and conferences in other industries. I learn more that way. I pick up ideas that I can cross-fertilize and bring into my work, which will help my customers.

Traditional industries are restrictive because they're based first on the products and services sold by their members. If they sell drugs, they're in the pharmaceutical industry. If they sell massage therapy, they're in the physiotherapy industry. If they sell insurance, they're in the insurance industry. The industry and the product/service are intertwined.

But in the New Economy, it makes more sense for companies to congregate around a particular type of customer. If we work with business owners, we're in the business owner marketplace. If we work with families, we're in the family marketplace. If we work with teenagers, we're in the teenager marketplace. (This may include parents, who know that raising teenagers is definitely an industrious activity.)

Congregating around the customer type, rather than a common product or service, makes sense on many levels. We'll meet other business people who have the same kinds of customers. We might be able to do cross-promotions and refer customers to one another. Few people are going to co-operate like that in a traditional industry because they compete with each other. In this new model, that's not the case. We have the same kind of customer but aren't selling the same thing.

For example, let's say two companies work with sports teams. One firm provides motivational training and the other sells insurance. They have the same customers but do completely different things. It's in their best interest to work together.

Relinquishing a slavish allegiance to an industry is also helpful because it gives a green light to transcend and integrate: Strategy No. 6. We stop battling the competition and realize we don't have any competition. By bringing together different resources, our companies become unique entities with much higher value propositions. For example, for the sport teams market, we could bring together a consortium that combines motivational training, insurance, scouting, AI analytics (think *Moneyball*), and promotional management. The new factory pulls from every possible old economy industry but isn't in any industry. It's unencumbered.

Strategy No. 23 is one of the hardest to pull off, but not due to some huge logistical roadblock. It's hard to pull off mentally. We tend to be attached to our industry affiliations. They give us a sense of community. We feel loyal to and protective of our industries. We might even be part of the industry hierarchy with its attendant perks and status. But in the New Economy, adherence to an industry is a trap that stops us from achieving full potential.

The best way to start with this strategy is to build a new factory. Our old factories will still belong to industries. No problem. But our new factories won't belong to any industry. They'll be designed solely to help our best customers in whatever way we can. We're liberated to range widely, to find resources and partners who come from any kind of traditional industry or product/service category.

Using Strategy No. 23, we have permission to be industry-free, and the best part is we don't have to abandon our existing industries. We can still attend industry conferences and compile designations and wall-mounted certificates. But now we're free. We'll also come to appreciate the fact that the idea of an industry is just a social construct. It's not actually a real thing. It's just a convenient, albeit increasingly irrelevant, way to organize things.

I've always believed in the power of the generalist. Back in high school, I hated meeting with guidance counsellors because they were always trying to pigeonhole me. They gave me a list of careers and told me to pick one. But I couldn't do it. It seemed too restricting. I wanted to keep my options open, but I worried about my future. I figured I needed to pick a specific profession or I'd end up living in a back alley.

When I look back on things, though, I recall that my favourite subject was geography. It was also my best subject. I loved geography because it was about everything. It wasn't just about geology; it was about economics, politics, culture, history, current affairs, language, and everything else. At the time, even though I loved the general nature of the subject, I thought it was a bit of a bird course and not particularly useful in the real world.

Now, I realize that the future belongs to the generalist. Those who are rigidly specialized risk being replaced by robots or changes in market forces, and if they lose their jobs or businesses, they won't have the resilience to pivot. But people who have a wide breadth of eclectic interests, knowledge, and experience have much better prospects in the New Economy. As things continuously change, generalists can pivot more adroitly. They're also able to combine previously unrelated elements into new inventions.

Old factory thinking conspires against generalists at a time when they're most needed. For the most part, our current culture values specialists and dismisses generalists as dilettantes who can't make up their minds. That's why Strategy No. 23, as with most of the strategies in this book, requires running counter to the current culture.

When it comes to escaping from the strictures of an industry, watch out for what I call the crab problem. What's the crab problem? Well, if we have a pot full of live crabs, we don't need a lid to keep them from escaping. They'll do the policing for us. If one of the crabs tries to climb out of the pot, the other crabs will reach up and pull it back in. That's what happens when people try to extricate themselves from an industry. The other crabs try to pull them back in. That's why they need friends on the outside. They need industry outsiders to pull them out of the pot.

So build new factories. Make it about customers, not about products or services. Have an open mind. Give permission to provide any kind of value. Stop hanging around with the other crabs. Get out, explore, and have a good time. It's actually a lot more fun outside the pot, especially when we realize why there's a pot in the first place, and why the temperature of the water is getting hotter.

STRATEGY NO. 24

Co-Create

THEY NEVER KNEW. In the weeks leading up to Christmas, I made it clear to my parents that I only wanted one present: the LEGO Mega-Building Box. At nine years old, I was a rabid LEGO fan. My lobbying efforts were intense because I didn't want a repeat of the previous year's Yuletide letdown when my folks, still ridiculously posing as Santa, gave me a typewriter. I mean, who gives their eight-year-old kid a typewriter for Christmas? I wanted a road-race set, but instead I got a lousy typewriter. I might have become a Formula 1 racer instead of a writer if my parents had only followed orders.

So that year I wasn't taking any chances. I went to the department store and found the exact LEGO box I wanted. I wrote down the product name, the price, and location in the store and handed the list to my mom. "This is what I want for Christmas, Mom," I said imperiously. "Don't screw it up."

On Christmas Eve, after my parents went to bed, I snuck down to the living room to see what Santa had left under the tree. Sure enough, I spied a big box. It was the requisite size and shape with a label that said: "To Bill, from Santa." Excited and unwilling to wait until morning, I gingerly removed the wrapping, opened the box, took out the LEGO blocks, and constructed a rudimentary model of the Apollo *Saturn V* rocket. (In addition to LEGO, I was also an ardent fan of the space program.) Eventually, I felt sated. Feeling a tad tawdry, I put everything back into the box carefully, rewrapped it, and returned to bed.

The next morning, I did my best to act surprised as I opened my LEGO gift from Santa. "It's exactly what I wanted!" I exclaimed, hugging my parents. "Thank you so much."

I've never told anyone that story, at least not in print. I'm not particularly proud of my deception on Christmas Eve, but I was only nine years old and simply loved LEGO. I thought it was one of the great toy products. But, of course, like most toys, my passion for LEGO waned when I entered the dark and tumultuous epoch otherwise known as teenage years (I'll cover those stories in another book.)

So why the heck am I writing about LEGO? Because it's a great example of Strategy No. 24: Co-Create. In the early 2000s, LEGO was in dire straits. The direction of the company was unclear. It had too many product lines and its operations were too complex and cumbersome. The company needed to do something bold to get it back on track, so it chose to co-create.

In 2004, LEGO sought help with product development from its customers. It launched two initiatives: LEGO Ideas and LEGO User Groups. Since then, more than a million people have submitted ideas for new LEGO products. When an idea is accepted, the inventor receives a percentage of the sales. Ironically, one of the ideas was a LEGO product for the Apollo *Saturn V* rocket, a more refined version of the one I surreptitiously constructed that Christmas Eve long ago.

LEGO's foray into co-creation paid off handsomely. Sales soared. Thousands of people, mostly adults, joined user groups around the world. The user groups meet to build LEGO together, like a knitting group or a bridge club. The company also built LEGO theme parks around the world and produced a series of successful LEGO movies. Recently, I played the LEGO Batman virtual reality game using Facebook's Oculus Quest headset. It's incredible.

In a New Economy way, LEGO revived its fortunes by enlisting the active participation of its customers in the re-creation of its business. In hindsight, that sounds like an obvious strategy, but it's not. Most companies still operate like impenetrable citadels cut off from their customers. When they develop new products, they do it in secret. Sure, they might hold focus groups and pick the brains of their customers, but the creative process is internal. They put together a new product or a new business and then spring it on the marketplace to see if people want it. But this is just gambling.

In the dance with robots, co-creation isn't only wiser, it's easier. Networks make it possible to crowdsource ideas and get product development feedback from customers. Digital technology gives us the tools to quickly and cheaply create prototypes — both tangible and intangible — to try out on our customers. In the early stages, we can see if our ideas are catching on, giving us the opportunity to pivot, which increases chances that our new ventures will be successful. By co-creating, we also nurture deeper, more engaged relationships with our customers.

Co-creation takes many forms. We can stage contests that challenge people to solve problems or invent something new, such as the XPRIZE started by entrepreneur Peter Diamandis. The winner of a contest of this nature typically receives a monetary reward.

Co-creation can also be an ongoing invitation for customers and inventors to submit their ideas. It can be done one-on-one with specific customers to solve their particular problems.

In my BIG Idea Adventure Program, we coach our members to use co-creation to refine their big ideas. During our initial sessions with them, we develop a working prototype we call Version 1. Our members try out their ideas on "guinea pigs" — existing customers they trust. The first test is to tell the story about a big idea. We want to see if the idea itself, presented verbally, resonates with the target market. Once we have a story that works, we create Version 2, which includes more tangible things like pictures, exercises, physical prototypes, and anything else the guinea pigs can look at, hold in their hands, or try out.

During these co-creation sessions, the guinea pigs help determine what works and what doesn't. We keep an open mind and try not to be attached to our original ideas. We hope the guinea pigs will reveal things we couldn't imagine ourselves.

As we work through each prototype, we get more confident and excited that we're on the right track. Sometimes we get a huge insight from co-creators that makes all the difference. For example, years ago I held a workshop at a business school about "digital marketing." Attendance was light, and I couldn't figure out what was wrong. It was during the height of the internet bubble in the 1990s. Curious about why my workshop wasn't selling, I decided to co-create a new version of it with clients. One of them said something that made all the difference: "Nobody knows what digital marketing is. You should call it the Internet Marketing Workshop." That was it. Swap out the word *digital* for the word *internet*. It was so obvious, but I couldn't see it on my own. I was hung up on the word *digital*. I thought it sounded more advanced. But my guinea pig was right. We changed the name and sold out all the seats at our next workshop.

View co-creation as a continuous process. Every time we meet with a customer, co-create. Go into a meeting with an open mind. Seek the advice and ideas of customers or prospects. Incorporate these ideas into the thinking to build solutions together.

Co-creation is the way I write my books. I come up with the spark of an idea. I think of a working name for the book. *Swimming with Robots*, for instance. I do a mock-up of the cover. I write a chapter or two. Then I co-create it. I send out my prototype book to the people in my network for feedback. I listen to what they say: "I'm not sure I get this swimming thing. Maybe something else. How about dancing? Why don't you call it *Dancing with Robots*?"

As the book progresses, I continue to seek ideas from my crowd and incorporate the best suggestions in the book: "Maybe it should be about strategies for the New Economy. Maybe a specific number of them. Maybe 12 or 20 or 29."

I used to think it was cheating to get help writing my books. If other people helped, how could I say I wrote it? But I got over that. I realized I just wanted the best book possible. I also learned it was more fun to have other people involved in the process. Co-creation also makes the book better.

A friend once counselled me: "If you ask someone for money, they'll give you advice. If you ask them for advice, they'll give you money."

This is the essence of co-creation. When we go out into the marketplace looking for advice, people will give us money. By basing our relationships on co-creation, our prospects and customers will feel heard, appreciated, and validated. They'll feel motivated to help us, both for altruistic reasons (most people love to help others) and for self-interest (the resulting co-creation will benefit them). And because they had a hand in creating the product or service, they'll buy it.

In the old economy, things changed slowly. The same product could be sold year after year. But in the New Economy, everything changes at light speed. Product life cycles have shrunk from years to months to days to nanoseconds. In fact, the idea of a product life cycle is obsolete. Co-creation replaces it. We work with our customers to continuously create new value with them, value that resonates with them in the moment. The next day, we co-create something else that fits that moment. It's a continuous, dynamic, and creative process that never ends. This might sound exhausting, but it's actually exhilarating. Every day, every moment, something new.

Co-creation is like LEGO. Find a partner, open up the box (on Christmas Day, not the night before), pull out the blocks, and start building something new. Enjoy the co-creation. Then, the next day, do it again. And then again and again. As a co-creator, like with LEGO, we never know what we'll build next.

STRATEGY NO. 25

Frame Everything Ethically

----

*Throughout our nervous history, we have constructed
pyramidic towers of evil, ofttimes in the name of good.*

— Maya Angelou

AS HENRY FORD pieced together his first automobile, did he imagine traffic accidents and drive-by shootings? While conceiving the special theory of relativity, did Albert Einstein have premonitions of Hiroshima or Chernobyl? What about the architects of the internet? Did they foresee the rise of teenage suicide or election interference? Probably not. Engrossed in the excitement of their inventions, they likely spent little or no time thinking about long-term implications.

Since the dawn of time, new technology has been a double-edge sword. I'm sure our ancestors were thrilled by the discovery of fire, that is until someone burned to death. Every invention has its downside. Every tool can be used for good or evil. The problem is that we tend to talk up the benefits of new technology while avoiding difficult discussions that might rain on the parade.

Rushing forward with new technology without considering downsides is foolhardy. We fail to put in place safeguards or oversight that might mitigate negative repercussions. We also pretend that our technocratic contributions have nothing to do with the harm they cause downstream. Hannah Arendt called this the banality of evil.

Consider robot manufacturers. Right now, robots are still pretty rudimentary. Think of them as Version 1 robots. They can vacuum a house and help run a factory, but right now they don't seem to pose a threat. But what will Version 10 robots be able to do? What effect will they have on our society? In Ian McEwan's novel *Machines Like Me*, the main character, Charlie, purchases Adam, a cutting-edge android designed to be his "intellectual sparring partner, friend, and servant." Things go well for Charlie at first. Adam is compliant, helpful, and fun to play with. But soon enough, Adam exerts unexpected influence on Charlie's life. Charlie has buyer's remorse. But it's too late. The genie is out of the bottle. I won't add any spoilers, but the outcome is deep, profound, and disturbingly negative.

Of course, our culture is replete with tales of technology gone wrong, from Mary Shelley's *Frankenstein* to *Blade Runner* to *The Matrix* to *The Terminator*. We get it. Robots are going to kill us all. But I think that's misrepresenting the threat. Robots aren't going to kill us, but they could enable us to kill ourselves. They might also cause all kinds of unnecessary misery.

That's why it's vital to employ Strategy No. 25: Frame Everything Ethically.

Ethical framing is one of our Human Superpowers. Robots don't have an ethical bone, or processor, in their bodies. We're born to live and breathe ethics. It's what makes us human. Every thought we have, every action we take, is based on our ethics. Sometimes our ethics are good, sometimes they're bad. Sometimes we live up to our ethics, sometimes we fail. But regardless, values and ethics reside in our cells. The trick is to recognize their importance.

In our technology-driven world, ethics take a back seat. New technology is created and promulgated without a single discussion about ethics. We typically wait until something bad happens before we question the ethical drawbacks of a new gizmo. But by then it's too late.

The internet is a case in point. The tentacles of the network reach into every aspect of our lives. The internet has reached the point where we can't live with it and we can't live without it. So when we see that social media is undermining democracy, we can't solve the problem by disconnecting the internet. When we see that the Russians can hack and disrupt the West, we can't ban them from the network. We have to live with these issues and figure out how to manage them. We have to frame these problems from an ethical perspective and act accordingly.

Algorithms are an example of how technology fosters ethical ambiguities. They make it easier for companies and organizations to analyze data and make decisions. But they can also exacerbate inequality, racism, and social injustice. Once again, we have to look at algorithms from an ethical perspective. How can we use them, change them, and manage them so they do no harm?

Facial recognition is another example. It's very useful for security purposes. It can help catch criminals and terrorists, but it can also be used for social control.

Dictators, autocrats, and unethical business people love these technologies. They see how they can use them for nefarious ends. But what about us, the good guys? How do we make sure we win, that good prevails?

We need to bring ethics to the forefront in our discussions about technology and the future. The first question shouldn't be: What can this technology do? Rather, the question should be: Is this technology going to help people or hurt people?

But that's the bare minimum. We also have to look at how a new technology fits into the overall network and what cumulative effect all of these technologies working together will have on our society and our economy. How will they affect people?

We think we can tame technology, but that's a delusion. Technological progress has its own volition.

That's why we must start with ethics. What do we really want? What kind of world do we want to build? How can we maximize the good and minimize the bad?

Perhaps there are some technologies we shouldn't build. In 2015, a host of experts, including Stephen Hawking and Elon Musk, advised that research should be conducted into the societal impact of artificial intelligence.

Hawking and Musk warned that the rise of AI could signal the end of the human race. Hawking also counselled against trying to contact alien civilizations. He thought it a good idea to keep Earth a galactic secret in case some aliens might see our blue planet as a tasty morsel.

Ethical framing is now critical to the ongoing viability of every company and organization. In the old economy, companies could keep politics and social issues separate from their business operations. My dad told me: "Never talk politics or religion with customers."

But today, our customers assess our ethics and values. If we match their values, they buy from us. If we don't match their values, they don't buy from us. And it doesn't work to keep our values a secret. They see silence as complicity.

I'm talking, of course, about cancel culture. The internet and social media spawned cancel culture. Some see it as a form of mob repression, others see it as a tool to promote social justice. But regardless of its merits, cancel culture makes ethical framing more important than ever.

Like it or not, we need to pick a side. We need to think deeply about our ethics and values. What do we really believe in? What's important to us? Then we need to stand up for those values by embedding them in our company. We need to communicate them to our customers and walk the talk.

Remember that companies are part of a global network. Even if we don't use Twitter or Instagram, our companies aren't separate from the network. In an instant, our organizations could become embroiled in a social media maelstrom. If that happens, we better have our ethical houses in order.

Authenticity is critical. The network community can tell easily if a company uses societal issues as a marketing ploy. The community doesn't like greenwashing (pretending to care about the environment when nothing tangible is done about it) or virtue signalling (when token support for a cause is posted but nothing substantial is done to support it, nor does the poster really care about it).

It's helpful to think of the internet as a biological entity. It's an interconnected network of cells and organs. Ideas enter the organism. Some of these ideas are like viruses that quickly multiply. The organism then introduces other ideas that act as antibodies. Sometimes the virus wins, but most of the time, if the organism has taken care of itself, the malevolent virus is snuffed out. And like any organism, this is a continuous process. Ethical framing is a way to strengthen an immune system and fight off viruses if they attack on the network.

Ethical framing is also a driver of innovation. If we begin by thinking about who we want to help (Strategy No. 2), with an emphasis on the intention to help, then we'll think deeply about what it means to be "helpful." Is it good enough to help people enjoy a momentary pleasure of consumption while also contributing to the degradation of the environment or the society? That's why Strategy No. 1 is Achieve Well-Being Using Fewer Resources. If our intention is to help people achieve greater well-being, we'll look deeper at the ethical implications of what we're doing. This ethical framing will give us new ideas for potentially lucrative innovations.

In the New Economy, business isn't just business. I've been disheartened to meet business people who don't care what they do as long as they make money. Making money is their only value. But what profits people if they gain the whole world but lose their souls? It doesn't seem that such people care. But now they need to care. The network is watching. It wants to know what they believe in.

That's why I'm encouraged about the New Economy from an ethical standpoint. The transparency demanded by the network drives ethical behaviour. Certainly, there are problems with cancel culture and internet mobs. People and companies are wrongly condemned, and the punishment doesn't always fit the crime, but robots are actually helping to bend the moral arc of the universe toward justice. If companies are more accountable for their ethical conduct, they'll be more ethical, not because they're necessarily good but because it's in their best interest to be good.

Ethical framing is in our best interest. It's good for our souls, but it's also good for business. Perhaps we can work with robots, not to foster a banality of evil but to cultivate a banality of good. It's our choice.

STRATEGY NO. 26

Stop Working So Hard

THEY LAUGHED WHEN I brought a book to work. It almost got me fired. But my boss, Bruno, a boisterous behemoth of a man, understood. He said: "Leave Bishop alone. He figured out how to get the job done in half the time, so let him read his book. He earned it."

I've been a bookworm since the age of five. I've had a book on the go, sometimes multiple books, every day for the past 60 years. I'll read the back of a box of detergent if there's nothing else around. So when I got a job as a dishwasher the worst part was that I couldn't read while I was washing dishes. I operated an industrial-strength Hobart pass-through dishwasher. I loaded the dirty dishes in front and then retrieved the clean ones on the other end.

In concept, the job was a nightmare — never-ending dishes, pots, glasses, cups, and cutlery. My employer, a large food service company, had trouble keeping dishwashers. They went through two or three per week. Everyone hated the job. But I decided to make the most of it. I figured out how I could spend half the time doing dishes and the rest reading my book.

(It turned out I was the company's first porcelain cleanliness technician who had ever had literary ambitions.)

During my training, I took a hard look at the process the company promoted. Basically, the idea was to stuff dishes into the machine willy-nilly as they were being off-loaded in the "dish pit" by busboys. The busboys rushed back and forth haphazardly, perpetually loading and off-loading. The dishwasher was run off his or her feet. It was exhausting.

After the trainer left, I took another approach. When the busboys arrived with the dishes, I organized them on a side table. I placed the dirty dishes in organized stacks and groupings. Then, when I had enough, I loaded a single category of dishes into the machine. I then breezily strolled to the end of the machine, removed the dishes from the off-loader, and stacked them neatly on the shelves. So much better. The process was more relaxing and cut down the time required by more than 50 percent. On my off-time, I whipped out my book (appropriately on that first day, *Of Human Bondage* by Somerset Maugham).

Of course, I lived in fear that the authorities would catch me reading my book and snatch it away from me, or fill up my idle time with some other menial task. I suspected they might reward my increased efficiency by giving me more work to do. But Bruno saved me. He either appreciated my inventiveness, or he secretly admired my bibliophile nature, or he thought *Of Human Bondage* was a Marxist-Leninist tract calling for the overthrow of capitalism, but regardless, he came to my defence and let me read my book.

Bruno didn't know it, but he was a new economist. He intuitively understood Strategy No. 26: Stop Working So Hard.

In the New Economy, hard work isn't valued anymore. That might sound like a bad thing, a dismissal of the Protestant work ethic, but it's actually a good thing. Strenuous labour isn't valued because robots are better at it. One robot can do the labour of a thousand people. Robots never get tired and they don't take bathroom breaks. They don't ask for raises; in fact, they don't even want salaries, benefits, or pensions. That's why I wrote this book. Robots will replace traditional labour. It's inevitable. So we can't compete with robots by working hard; we have to take a different approach. We need to follow new strategies. We need to stop working so hard.

That doesn't mean we get lazy or lie around reading books all day long (I'll make an exception in the case of this book, though). It just means we have to find new ways to provide value that don't involve time and effort.

I recommend we set this goal: double our income and work 50 percent less time. If we work toward that objective, we'll have to innovate and transcend the traditional definition of human labour. It forces us to do something radically different.

We could probably double our income. We just have to double the hours we work. We could also work 50 percent less time, but we might lose income. But if we want to double our income and work 50 percent less, we have to do something new. We can't do it incrementally. We have to come up with something much different.

During the past decades, humans have tried to compete with robots by working harder. As the value of labour dropped or remained stagnant, hard-pressed workers worked longer hours just to keep up. They took on two, even three jobs. Once we had one-income families. Now have two-income or multi-income families. Even more insidious, we've become slaves to our robots. As they become faster and more powerful, we can't keep up with the demands they make on us. We endlessly labour to process a digital flood of emails, texts, and social media posts. The technology we thought would save us time, actually makes our lives busier and more stressful.

That's why we need a new perspective. In the New Economy, we get paid for results (Strategy No. 17). Nobody cares, or should care, about how hard we work. It's not about time and effort. I had a boss once, not as enlightened as Bruno, who was a nitpicker about punctuality. He flipped a bird if I came in one minute late. He also expected everyone to stay long after 5:00 p.m. He was hung up on productivity and measured our output based primarily on the hours we worked. He wasn't a fun guy to work for.

Unfortunately, most of us are still stuck in time-and-effort mode. Most employers still enforce strict time requirements. And even if we're self-employed, we might impose arduous regimens on ourselves. We might judge our own performances based on how long and hard we work, not on the results we achieve. That's the major reason we tend to work too hard. It's not that robots conspire against us; it's that our old factory minds tell us to work hard.

So don't work so hard. Think about how to get better results with less time and effort. Remember Strategy No. 1: Increase Well-Being Using Fewer Resources. We don't just do that for our customers; we also do it for ourselves.

Once we put our minds to it, doubling our income and working 50 percent less time isn't actually that hard to figure out when we activate the creative parts of our brains. Here's just a short list of things to work on:

- Develop higher-value products and services with higher-profit margins. If hot dogs are being sold, start selling gourmet meals.
- Teach people how to do things rather than do things for them.
- Package and sell intellectual property.
- Create online courses and digital content that can be bought and consumed without personal involvement.
- Delegate, automate, or eliminate low-value activities.
- Spend most of the time on high-value activities.
- Get robots to do the grunt work.

To get to the point where we can stop working so hard, we actually need to work harder first. This is a major roadblock we have to get over. We might feel we're too busy to create a gourmet business, or too stressed to update our systems. But this line of thinking keeps us stuck. We might have to work extra hours for the time being, but it's for a good cause. For example, if we spend an hour creating a more efficient system to manage our email, that extra hour will save us 1,000 hours in the future. If we spend the next month creating a more premium product or service, we'll be able to work fewer hours in the future and make more money.

Strategy No. 26 is the reason I created The Big Idea Adventure Program. Back in the 1990s, I worked long hours and didn't make a lot of money. I calculated I worked 70 hours per week and made about $75 per hour. After overhead costs, that didn't leave very much in my pocket. So I made it my goal to double my income and only work 35 hours per week. To get there, I had to think differently. The solution couldn't be about brute force. It couldn't be about doing more marketing projects. I had to think about more transcendent value.

With these principles in mind, I began to think of myself as a "marketing plumber." Like a plumber, I did projects by the hour. My value proposition was based primarily on my labour. I decided to become a "marketing architect" and get paid for my experience, knowledge, and creativity. I would get paid for big ideas.

Becoming a marketing architect was the right move. By building my value proposition around something intangible — big ideas — I was no longer tied to time and effort. It was all about results.

Since I started the program, I work less time and make more money. I far and away exceeded my original expectations. I also do much more enjoyable and meaningful work and have a much greater impact in the world.

One experience made me glad that I stopped working so hard. I had a client who sold investments in real estate. He struggled to sell his investment opportunities — the minimum investment was $10 million. To develop a new sales strategy, he paid me $15,000 upfront for five big idea sessions. After the first session, he called me and said that he didn't need to do the other four sessions. I was concerned he wasn't happy and that he wanted a refund, but it was the opposite. He was thrilled. "Bill, the big idea you gave me in the first session worked like a charm. I sold $30 million in investments using it. So I don't need to do the other sessions. I'm good."

I did a calculation. The session we did together was three hours. That meant he paid me $5,000 per hour, yet he was happy because he sold $30 million in investments based on my idea. My client didn't care how long it took me. He just wanted results.

Stop working so hard. It's a trap. Make it your goal to double your income and work 50 percent less time. Decide what you really want to do (like read a book), then organize your work (like washing dishes), so you can do it. And get robots to help.

STRATEGY NO. 27

Smarten Up

MY TELLTALE-HEART STORY began when my wife, Ginny, flew off to Hawaii for a 10-day conference. It was my chance to install a smart thermostat in our house. I knew Ginny would be against it — she liked our simple old-school thermostat — but I knew, being a robot-kind-of-guy, that a smart thermostat was a great idea. It promised to cut our electricity bill in half and save the planet by learning our lifestyle habits and optimizing our energy use. I was sure Ginny would embrace the smart thermostat after it was in operation.

When she returned from Hawaii, Ginny wasn't pleased with my unilateral decision, but she agreed to give the smart thermostat a chance.

Things went well the first week. The furnace hummed along. The smart thermostat kept us warm in the morning, lowered the temperature during the day when we were at work, and pumped it back up in the evening. I was excited that the thermostat was "learning." It monitored our lifestyle and adjusted its programming.

But in the second week, things went haywire. The furnace came on and went off at odd hours. It was cold when it should have been warm, and warm when it should have been cold.

Eventually, I figured out the problem. The smart thermostat was confused because we aren't a typical family. We work at home some days and at the office at other times. We have a cabin we visit every two weeks. We have a housekeeper that comes and goes. Another person comes in to check on our cat.

Our lifestyle is very chaotic, so the thermostat couldn't figure out what to do. In short order, it had a robotic nervous breakdown. I could tell a major "I told you so" was in the offing. So I decided to un-smart the thermostat that we had come to call HAL, from the movie *2001: A Space Odyssey*. Just as in the film, I removed the thermostat's core intelligence functions, leaving it with a very low IQ.

After I received my well-earned "I told you so," I begrudgingly agreed to ditch HAL and reinstall our old thermostat. It felt like a retreat — especially for a New Economy guy like me — but in the interest of domestic harmony, I got out my tools and retired HAL to my big box of "technology that didn't fly."

That was a few years ago. Funny to say, we still get email reports from HAL trying to inform us about our energy consumption. I liken HAL to the telltale heart from the story by Edgar Allan Poe where a murderer is eternally haunted by the beating heart of his victim, who he had buried under the floorboards in his house.

HAL is an example of my many forays into the world of SMART devices. I love gadgets, and smart gadgets are the best ones. Today, we have smart everything: smart refrigerators, smart ovens, smart watches, smartphones, and smart cities. We even have smart commanders that coordinate all of our smart devices.

SMART stands for self-monitoring analysis and reporting technology. Initially, smart devices were used to monitor and respond to problems inside computer systems, but gradually branched out into thousands of devices. We now have smart devices and dumb devices (or to be nice, let's call them not-so-smart devices). Smart devices augur much promise, but as in the case of HAL, some of them are still a work in progress. Others are of dubious merit, such as the smart toothpick or the smart bowling ball.

Regardless, the New Economy could be renamed the "Smart" Economy. New technology is making it feasible to transform any device into a smart device. I work with a company that builds and installs smart traffic signs. Their smart stop sign, for example, has sensors that report remotely if it needs repair. Another client sells smart sensors for grain silos. In both cases, the smart devices are connected to a master server that uses algorithms to interpret and report on the data it receives.

While turning dumb devices into smart devices is a powerful trend in the New Economy, the need to "smarten up" can be applied to any kind of business. A device isn't needed to do that. A service business, for instance, can be turned into a "smart" service business. In fact, it's an imperative. In the New Economy, it's no longer feasible to run a basic business. The marketplace is complex, and there's a lot of competition.

Imagine a distribution company. Generally speaking, it's a simple business. Products are sourced and then distributed to customers. But today a basic distributor is wiped out a by smart competitor who has more sophisticated systems. The smart competitor provides much faster fulfillment and even predicts what's needed before customers know themselves. The distribution company links its business systems to the business systems of its customers, ensuring that unnecessary inventory is never held while always being able to meet its customers' needs.

Imagine a company that rents out tractor trailers. A dumb version of the company simply provides the tractor trailers to trucking companies and has a yard full of its fleet standing idle to rent. But a smart version of the company goes much further. The tractor trailers have onboard sensing equipment to track their location, usage, maintenance, and motion experience. The smart company can give its clients reports on usage and efficiency. It can also go further to create the Airbnb of tractor trailer companies. Its platform enables trucking companies to rent out tractor trailers to other trucking companies.

Imagine a physiotherapy practice. It can be run as a simple business that provides hourly therapeutic sessions, but it could also be a smart physiotherapy business. The smart version could create an advanced health and wellness program incorporating a suite of therapeutic modalities such as aromatherapy, mindfulness meditation, and acupuncture.

In the New Economy, it's not just about doing something better; it's about doing something smarter. Someone could be the best massage therapist in the world but could be wiped out by a smart-enabled competitor.

That's why Strategy No. 27 is Smarten Up.

Over the holidays one year, Ginny purchased a gift online from a department store. It promised to deliver the present before Christmas, but the package never arrived. When she called to inquire about the delay, she couldn't get hold of anyone. She sent them a message online but got no response. Maddeningly, the department store charged her credit card but never delivered the gift. She tried to no avail to get the credit-card charge reversed. It was a nightmare.

Compare that to my experience with Amazon. I ordered Apple Airpods on a Monday, and the box arrived on Tuesday. But there was nothing in the box. I got someone on the line immediately who agreed to send me a replacement, which arrived on Wednesday. Amazon didn't give me a hard time. It didn't think I was lying. The company just replaced the product. It was incredible.

So which company do we want to work with going forward: the not-so-smart department store or Amazon? Everyone bemoans the demise of the old department stores, and many people vilify Amazon, but Amazon is a smart company. It's light years ahead of its competitors. It works endlessly to make itself smarter. That's why Jeff Bezos has a big yacht and takes trips into space. His company has a smarten-up attitude.

The master model for a SMART device is helpful for any company that wants to smarten up. There are four elements. One, a smart device/company is connected to the network. It's not standalone. Two, a smart device/company is aware. It constantly gathers information using robot sensors or human-embodied pattern recognition or both. Three, it analyzes that data and draws insights from it. And four, it's responsive. It makes changes and upgrades its operations when necessary.

The SMART model can be applied to devices, companies, and individuals. We, too, can be SMART humans. That doesn't mean we have to possess a high IQ; it means we bring into play the four SMART elements: connected data gathering, analysis, insight, and responsiveness. We constantly observe, think, learn, and respond.

The stakes are high. Recently, I subscribed to Apple Fitness+. The service provides online fitness classes that I can access through my iPhone, iPad, or Apple TV. It's also connected to my Apple Watch. While I do a class, my watch actively monitors my heart rate and displays it on the screen. It monitors my activity each day and provides historical reports.

Compare the Apple system to regular fitness clubs and typical online fitness instructors. They might have better fitness classes, but the Apple smart system goes well beyond classes. It costs about $15 per month, plus the price of an Apple Watch. So the traditional fitness industry won't be able to compete with Apple if it doesn't do something to smarten up.

The growing divide between the regular economy and the smart economy will widen. Primarily because the smart get smarter, but also because most companies these days don't think they need to smarten up, or they don't know it's an issue.

Don't be one of the dum-dums.

A useful way to smarten up is to think about your value proposition in two parts. I call this above-the-line, below-the-line. Take a blank piece of paper and draw a horizontal line through the centre. Below the line, jot down what your business currently does. Write a detailed description. Now look at the top of the page and contemplate what you can do to smarten up your business. Concentrate first on smart solutions you could provide to your customers. Write these ideas above the line. Then add ideas to smarten up your operations. Keep doing this exercise. Smart ideas will emerge.

Another helpful analogy is the LED light bulb. Below the line is a regular light bulb, the kind that's been around for more than a century since Thomas Edison invented it. Above the line is an LED light bulb. It can cost 20 times more than a regular light bulb, but it's worth it. It lasts 10 years and uses much less energy. It's a smart light bulb that can be connected to a smart lighting system.

So what's your LED light bulb? How can you smarten up your products and services? How can you smarten up your business? How can you team up with robots to do it?

In the New Economy, the impetus toward smart is inexorable and far-reaching. Every industry and area of our lives will become smart. Everything will be connected, aware, analytical, and responsive. There will be fits and starts in the smarten-up revolution (my HAL thermostat is still haunting me from the grave). But that's just growing pains.

Eventually, smart devices will become invisible. We won't notice them or find them remarkable, in the same way we don't marvel at our television. Smart devices will be unobtrusive, just part of our lives. Smart companies will be better run and more profitable. Smart people will be kinder, happier, and more fulfilled.

So get above the line and smarten up.

STRATEGY NO. 28

Connect with Nature

IN THE FOREST clearing, I came across a blackened pile of rusty appliance parts. It looked like the remains of a washing machine that had been ripped apart and torched during some kind of midnight satanic ritual. It was identical to a dozen other fire sites I'd found in the forest on our log cabin property. Each one of the blackened sites had piles of garbage — car parts, tin cans, even a bathroom scale — that had been burned.

After talking to neighbours, I learned that the previous owner was notorious for his "war against nature." Not only did he like to burn appliance parts, he spent weekends hunting down animals on the property: deer, racoons, squirrels, rabbits, possums, and porcupines. Not to mention birds: wild turkeys, pheasants, blue jays, orioles, woodpeckers, and hawks. His killing sprees accounted for the hundreds of shotgun casings we found scattered over the property. He'd also taken a dislike to flora and was known to deliberately ram his tractor into trees, scarring the bark. He was also a fire risk and lit huge bonfires during fire bans. Scary guy.

The neighbours were relieved that we purchased the property. I told them we considered ourselves to be stewards with a sacred duty to care for the flora and fauna. We promised to heal the property and return it to its natural balance.

It was a remarkable experience. When we bought the cabin, the place was dead silent, but not in a good way. I mean, dead silent. There were no birds or animals. There weren't even any bees or butterflies. They had long ago fled the battlefield. But over time, the creatures returned. The sound of chirping birds resumed. Rabbits came hopping across the lawn. Even the stock of trout in the pond multiplied. Natural harmony was restored.

We often speculate about the previous owner's mental state. Was he a crazy dude? Did he have anger issues? We wondered why he took out his frustrations on nature. But I also knew he wasn't an outlier. Many people take a confrontational approach to nature. They think they're separate from it, that nature is something to be conquered, exploited, even destroyed. Of course, this is terrible for those of us who love our planet, but it's also bad business. In the case of our cabin's previous owner, his war on nature cost him money. We bought the place at a big discount because no one wanted to buy it. The place looked like a disaster zone. I bought it because I had experience reclaiming distressed and run-down properties, but most real estate buyers are repelled by a place in such derelict condition. Because of his war on nature, he lost a hundred grand or more.

That's why Strategy No. 28 is Connect with Nature.

In the New Economy, it pays to connect with nature. It's not just a tree-hugging, leftist, Green Party thing; it's good business. By connecting a business with nature, we not only help save the planet, we create more value and wealth in the world. And we get robots to help.

But before we get into the opportunities, let's delve into the past. For the past million years or more, we've been at odds with nature. It's understandable. Our poor cave-dwelling ancestors were bedevilled by nature. They were eaten by tigers, plagued by disease, roasted by heat, and frozen by cold. To survive, humans had to win the war with nature. So we used our inventive minds to wage this battle. We learned how to kill animals more efficiently, combat disease, and extract resources from the earth for our profit and pleasure. We achieved dominion over nature.

Our adversarial stance toward nature is deep-seated in our collective conditioning. The previous owner of my cabin was simply channelling this aggression. But he's not the only one. Generally speaking, most businesses in the old economy were based on the same aggression. The whole point of the Industrial Revolution, if you think about it, was to mechanize the war on nature. And it was profitable. And it was also beneficial in many ways. Billions of people were lifted out of poverty by the Industrial Revolution. But, of course, like most things in life, this "progress" has a downside. We're in danger of destroying the environment that serves as the foundation of our economy. Consider the economic costs of climate change. Consider the negative impact on business caused by Covid-19, which some scientists say was caused by urban encroachment on the natural world.

By placing us in an adversarial relationship, the Industrial Revolution made us feel disconnected from nature. We took our collective cues from René Descartes and Isaac Newton who popularized a mechanistic world view, the belief that the universe was simply a big machine that we could understand completely and control absolutely. God created this machine, they postulated, and put us in control of it as masters of the universe.

In the New Economy, this mechanistic cosmology, and its attendant ego-driven belief that nature is our servant, is crumbling. It no longer makes practical sense, business sense, or spiritual sense. As we become more connected with ourselves through the network and more connected with robots, it makes more sense to also connect with nature. This idea runs counter to the current fears of connective technology, that it will further alienate us from nature.

As we become more connected using the internet, we have the profound experience of being more connected in general. I see it in my kids. They grew up in a connected social environment mediated by technology such as Facebook, Twitter, and Instagram. They know what it feels like to be connected. In fact, to them, being connected is like being a fish in water. Connection is the medium they swim in, and they don't know anything different. It's easier for me to see the difference, coming from an older generation that grew up in a hierarchical social structure mediated by top-down technology like radio and TV.

Being acclimatized to connection, the new generation of humans are more inclined to be connected to nature. My son and his partner left urban life to start an organic farm. Their farming philosophy is built on the idea of connecting more deeply with nature, to grow food using less mechanistic and aggressive techniques. For example, they don't use machines to till the soil. They avoid disturbing the soil. They nurture it. And as a result, their food is better than old economy food. I've never tasted such delicious and nutritious tomatoes, squash, onions, and carrots. As such, by connecting with nature more deeply than their old economy competitors, they can sell their produce at a premium.

Connecting with nature makes great economic sense for every kind of company. As we discussed with Strategy No. 7: Dematerialize, companies have a financial incentive to extract less from the earth. It lowers their input costs. They also have an incentive to decrease their use of energy. It reduces their overhead. They also have an incentive to increase well-being using fewer resources (Strategy No. 1), because it makes their products and services more marketable.

Companies in the New Economy also have an incentive to embrace what's called "the circular economy." In this economy, a company is no longer structured as a linear entity that draws a straight line from resource extraction through value creation to disposal of waste. Essentially, the old economy model is to take something out of the ground, do something with it, and then put it back in the earth as waste. That seems a bit nonsensical when we step back and look at it. Why would we want to throw away all those resources on the back end? Isn't it better to use those waste resources again, either for our own use or for another company to utilize as an input? That's the circular economy. We organize our business so that someone else's waste is our input and our waste is someone else's input. Once again, this approach not only helps Mother Nature, it bolsters the bottom line.

Robots can be our partners in connecting with nature. They can help us organize the circular economy. They can find circle partners and help us develop products, services, and processes that require less stuff from the earth (dematerialization).

Production processes are also made much more efficient and energy-efficient with robots. In the agricultural sector, robots (drones, sensing devices, and algorithms) enable precision planting, fertilizing, and harvesting. As a result, yields increase while decreasing the use of pesticides and fertilizer. In every manufacturing and service business, robots can perform a similar beneficial function. They can be our partners in connecting with nature.

In the New Economy, it's vital to appreciate the growing appetite of consumers for products and services that are good for the environment. The younger generation is much more aware of what impact brands have on the environment. Younger people share what they've learned on social media. They boycott companies that are nature-bashers. We might not care that much about the environment, but increasingly our customers do.

It's also useful to realize that our companies and ourselves are actually part of nature, not disconnected from it. A few years ago, I went on a month-long pilgrimage to India. We retraced the life of the Buddha, travelling across northern India from Delhi to places such as Sarnath, Varanasi, Bodh Gaya, and up into Nepal. It was an epic journey.

On a mountaintop called Vulture Peak, near a town named Rajgir, I learned that I'm not only connected to nature, I am nature. We were taught a parable by the Buddha called *The Heart Sutra*. It concerns the Buddhist principle of Not-Self, which proposes that the idea of self is an illusion, that everything is connected, that we're not just part of nature, we are nature. Maybe I was just caught up in spiritual excitement, but at that moment it all made sense to me. I am nature.

Upon my return to Toronto, I thought about how to apply this philosophy to the operation of my business. What would happen if I viewed my business as not only connected to nature, but as nature itself? How would that change things? The more deeply I contemplated this idea, the more apparent this reality became. My business wasn't a thing; it was a process. It wasn't separate from its environment; it was connected to it. I couldn't have my business without everything that it was connected to. It was also fluid. Nothing about my business ever stood still. You couldn't grab on to it. That would be like trying to hold on to a river by seizing a fistful of water as it rushes by. My business is just an idea. It doesn't exist in any real, tangible form. It's not the desks and computers. It's not the bank account. It's an idea driven by an intention to help people.

I also realized with excitement that robots were my allies in connecting. They enabled me to connect more deeply with people and provide more value to them. Robots gave me more tools to help people as well as new ways to increase value while using fewer resources. Put to these wholesome tasks, robots, I realized, could be used to make the world a better place.

I'm glad I took over the cabin property. The previous owner was infected with the idea of nature as an adversary. Why he bought a nature reserve, I don't know, but maybe he was trying to work something out. It was ironic to me that most of the detritus from his fires were artifacts of the industrial era — consumer products and machine parts. Perhaps he was trying to reconcile two opposing demons, attempting to seek dominance over nature that he saw as the enemy and his disgust with the Industrial Revolution and its negative impact on nature. Perhaps in his own weird way, he sided with nature.

This internal conflict is playing out in the economy. We want to be masters of the universe and we want to be good stewards of the earth. How we reconcile this paradox will be one of the most interesting things to watch as we go forward.

STRATEGY NO. 29

Be Human

WHO WOULD THINK that the stirrup would stir things up so dramatically? Around 6,000 years ago on the grasslands of the Eurasian steppes, someone clever got a big idea: instead of eating horses, he or she would employ them as a form of transportation. As can be imagined, these early horsemen (you can bet they were all men) used their equine transport to engage in all sorts of mayhem. Given their superior equine speed, they could attack a town, do a little afternoon pillaging, and then make a hasty retreat, outpacing their enraged victims who could only pursue them on foot.

Of course, everyone quickly caught on to the idea, and the age of the mounted horse was born. Warriors on horseback battled across Asia for thousands of years. Then, around 1600 BCE, someone in the Syrian army research department got the idea for the chariot. Just add a horse, Charlton Heston, and you've got Ben-Hur. Another step forward in warfare.

Chariots had advantages and disadvantages. It was easier to train some-one to drive a chariot. They could also accommodate two passengers, a driver, and someone to shoot arrows and throw spears. But chariots lacked manoeuvrability. In the heat of battle, someone on a horse could pivot much easier than someone in a chariot. Chariots were also expensive to manufacture and maintain. After every battle, they had to be taken to the shop for repairs and a tune-up.

Around 200 CE, someone came up with a simple, elegant idea that historians say changed the world: the stirrup. Using a simple strap of leather attached to the saddle (the saddle was a pretty good idea, too), the stirrup optimized mounted warfare. The stirrup made it easier to get up on a horse, especially when weighed down by armour. It also made riders more stable. They could be more accurate and deadly with their swords and bows.

In the Middle Ages, the stirrup gave knights in armour the stability to ride horses while brandishing three-metre-long lances. This turned horses and riders into medieval tanks that simply rolled over their less-endowed rivals. It also helped knights accrue tremendous political and social power. To maintain their legions of knights, kings gave them land and authority, creating a power structure that led to the rise of feudalism.

Dr. Lynn White, in his book *Medieval Technology and Social Change*, writes:

> Few inventions have been so simple as the stirrup, but few have had so catalytic an influence on history. The requirements of the new mode of warfare which it made possible found expression in a new form of western European society dominated by an aristocracy of warriors endowed with land so that they might fight in a new and highly specialized way.… The Man on Horseback, as we have known him during the past millennium, was made possible by the stirrup.…

The story of the stirrup is a lesson for us all. When new technology emerges, we don't usually think about how it will change the world. We focus on its utility. I'm sure the first person who used stirrups was very excited. He probably thought about how many more villages he could pillage. I'm positive he wasn't thinking the stirrup would have profound socio-economic implications. He just headed out for some mayhem with added gusto.

That's why I wrote this book — to get a conversation going about the New Economy and where it's headed. How will technology like AI and the blockchain affect our economy and our society? Before we mount the horse, we might want to pause for a second to think about where we want to ride it. But even more important, we need to think about how all this technology is going to affect us, how it's going to change us as humans.

The horseman with the stirrup was a different human than the one without it. He had more power. He could ride farther. He could carry more equipment. He could dominate those without stirrups. This fundamentally altered his self-image. It expanded what he believed was possible. It realigned how he related to other people. He became a new kind of human.

Think about it. Are we not different people because we now carry smartphones around with us all day? Aren't we different people because we use social media? Those maniacs who stormed the U.S. Capitol in Washington, D.C., weren't only driven to violence by social media but were changed as human beings by it. In some ways, they were like any violent mob in history — out of control and beyond reason — but their unique world view was formed by the interconnected and belief-bubble-forming nature of the internet.

Imagine how AI might change us as humans. For some of us, it will make us feel more powerful. It's kind of exhilarating to turn on the lights in a house by commanding Alexa to do it. We feel like a god. But who's really the deity? Us or Alexa?

As AI gets smarter and more ubiquitous, we might contract an inferiority complex. Even if we had an IQ of 140, we'd start feeling pretty stupid if we hung around with an Einstein all day. Or even worse, imagine how dumb we'd feel using AI that's 1,000 times smarter than Einstein. We might need some serious psychotherapy.

In his book *Understanding Media: The Extensions of Man*, Marshall McLuhan says technology is best understood as an extension of ourselves. They're not just tools. A new technology is like adding a new limb to our bodies. It changes how we're constructed as humans and transforms us as humans. Each new technology makes us a different kind of human.

McLuhan's hypothesis can be viewed as a good thing. As we add more technology, we can become more capable, empowered, and free. We can use these new limbs to do things and go places we couldn't before. But what if we add too many limbs too fast? Every morning we wake up and a company like Microsoft or Google has attached a new limb to our bodies. What if we can't remove it? Now we've got so many limbs that we're stuck. We become some kind of modern-day mythological monster like the Hecatoncheires, which had 50 heads and 100 arms. The point is, if we blindly adopt technology without judgment and discernment, we might not like the kind of humans we become.

That's why Strategy No. 29 is Be Human. Put human beings first. Put yourself first, before technology. Be the master, not the slave.

Reflect: What do we believe in? What are our values? What kind of world do we want to live in? What kind of person do we want to be, both in sentiment and action?

Perhaps we want to be more connected. What does it really mean for us to be connected? Does it mean having 4,000 friends on Facebook? Or does it mean having meaningful intimate relationships with a few special people?

Perhaps we want to be kinder and more compassionate. Does that mean virtue signalling on Instagram or taking concrete action in the real world?

Perhaps we want to be more generous, more peaceful, more understanding and tolerant.

In the post-hierarchical, post-modern world of the New Economy, we don't have to accept a culturally prescribed template for what it means to be human. We're free to custom-design our own bespoke versions. That's a good thing and a bad thing. It's bad because the internet is swarming with malevolent people offering us their ready-made templates, complete with conspiracy theories and self-image avatars. We could be tempted to fill a void of self with one of these false idols.

It's a good thing, however, because we have the freedom today to create our own unique selves. We can become the unique kind of human we want to be, and the internet gives us a window into all the possibilities. We just need to take control of our humanity project and not let technology do it for us.

To protect our humanity from being co-opted by robots, we must guard against greed, hatred, and delusion. The first guy who saddled up with his new stirrups surely felt the allure of these three poisons. He likely envisioned amassing great wealth. He likely thought about how the stirrup could help him kill more people. And he likely had the delusion that the stirrup was going to make him really happy.

I like to think of myself as a good person (the jury is still out), but I'm willing to admit that technology often feeds my greed, hatred, and delusion. It's insidious. I download a new kind of software because I think it will help me get richer. I wallow in Twitterland and get enraged. And I think that technology is the ticket to happiness. So I have to be mindful. I have to watch how I'm reacting in my relationship with technology. Does it really make me feel better? Am I actually happier?

What will happen when we all get an Einstein 1000 robot? I can imagine some of us might feel a little greed. Perhaps we could get the robots to manage our arbitrage accounts while we play video games. Perhaps we can use it to get revenge on someone? Surely, the robot will make us happy, right?

Never in our history has it been more important to reflect on what it means to be human. There are hundreds of new technologies coming on stream. Each one is a stirrup. These stirrups will not only empower us, they'll affect us. They'll change the direction of our future.

They're also rivals for our livelihood and our place in the world. That's the reason it's so important to think about how we want to live and the person we want to be. Grounded in a firm understanding of our own humanity, we can use technology with greater wisdom. We can select what works for us, our family, our business, and our community.

The key is to be proactive, not reactive. Step forward as a human being. Let the robots know who's in charge.

CONCLUSION

They Shoot Horses, Don't They?

You know horses are smarter than people. You never
heard of a horse going broke betting on people.

— Will Rogers

IN 1908, THERE were more than 120,000 horses in New York City, more than 500 horses per square mile. It was said that a New Yorker would see and use more horses in a day than a rancher in Montana. Horses pulled trolleys, carriages, wagons, and fire trucks. The average New Yorker took five horse-driven trips each day. Few people imagined that in 10 short years only a handful of horses would remain, that the horses would be replaced by the internal combustion engine.

New Yorkers eagerly welcomed the advent of the automobile. Horseless carriages were cleaner and faster. They didn't leave behind a trail of urine and manure (more than 227,000 litres of urine and 1.3 million kilograms of manure each day). Of course, New Yorkers didn't foresee that Manhattan would one day be jammed with cars or that smog would fill their lungs.

They also didn't think about how many people would be disrupted by this new technology. In one decade, millions of jobs were wiped out: horse breeders, grain farmers, feed merchants, carriage manufacturers, buggy whip makers, coachmen, groomers, blacksmiths, street cleaners, and veterinarians. In 1890, there were 13,800 carriage manufacturers in the United States. In 1920, there were only 90.

So what happened to all the horses? As we might expect, after all their tireless work, they weren't given a hefty severance package and put out to pasture. Millions of horses were slaughtered in one of the largest animal massacres in history.

And yet, in some quarters, people refused to let go of their horses. In the First World War, the British sent horse-mounted troops into battle against machine guns and tanks. They were mowed down. In the face of this carnage, the British Army held fast to its belief in horses. Its massive horse-centric infrastructure, built up over a thousand years, resisted modernization. Britain's military didn't want to replace horses with tanks. It didn't want to see the writing on the wall. Its livelihood was built around horses, not tanks.

The moral of these two stories can help us skillfully navigate our current situation. On the one hand, we can eagerly embrace robots, just like New Yorkers welcomed the automobile. But we must bear in mind the impact robots will have on people who work in the old economy. In our era, humans are the horses being replaced by technology. What are we going to do with them. Shoot them?

On the other hand, do we resist the rise of robots in the same way the British Army resisted tanks? Do we send people into battle with the robots to be mowed down? That's not going to work.

We must face reality. The robots are coming. They're already here and they're not going away. They're also coming quickly. It took 15 years to replace horses with cars. This transition will happen much faster.

We must step up. We must harness our Human Superpowers and work in concert with robots. We also need to change how we think about business and the economy and follow the New Economy strategies outlined in this book.

To get started, here's a simple dancing-with-robots process.

Step 1: Decide Who We Want to Help — It's important to stay focused on people. Don't pick technology first. Start with humans. What type of person, company, or organization do we really want to help?

Step 2: Identify the Big Problem and the Big Goal — What problems do our customers have that no one's helping them to solve? What's a big goal we could help our customers achieve?

Step 3: What's the Big Solution? — How can we help our customers solve the big problem and achieve the big goal?

Step 4: What Technology Can Help Us Provide the Big Solution? — Review all available technology. Pick the best ones and combine them if necessary.

Step 5: Think Big, Start Small — Begin by imagining the biggest possible outcome, system, and platform, then take a small first step. Test out a concept. Learn and adapt. Then take another step. Learn and adapt again. Don't hesitate. In the New Economy, we need to be swift.

One of the key principles of this book is that technology is more than just a tool; it's a relationship. When a new technology is introduced, it has a pervasive impact. It changes the economy and the marketplace. We become different humans.

In the novel *They Shoot Horses, Don't They?* by Horace McCoy (and the 1969 film by Sydney Pollack), poor and out-of-work couples compete in a Depression-era dance marathon. Over several weeks, the contestants dance continuously (with short breaks) until only one couple is left standing. It's a gruelling story based on real dance marathons staged during the 1930s in California. The contestants are so desperate that they're willing to do anything to win the $1,000 prize.

They Shoot Horses, Don't They? is a story about greed and the exploitation of the vulnerable. The contestants feel they have no choice. They have to keep dancing. But only one couple walks away with the prize. The rest get nothing.

Don't let the dance with robots become a dance marathon. Don't make it about greed and exploitation.

It's my hope that the dance with robots will be about making the world a better place. That we, our businesses, and our families will prosper in the New Economy.

That everyone will prosper.

AFTERWORD

Tentacles

MY LIFE HAD a gaping hole in it. People thought I had everything: youth, health, and wealth. But there was a void. That's why I got out of bed at 3:00 a.m. and boarded an all-night bus headed downtown to the Rotund Retail Centre.

When I arrived, I was astonished to discover that a lineup of shoppers snaked around the block and far down a back street. I reckoned at least 2,000 people had arrived ahead of me.

It was predicted that the XT9000 would break sales records. It boasted a legion of revolutionary capabilities and featured significant upgrades from its predecessor: the RC8000. Waiting impatiently in the queue, my body quaked with excitement. Soon an XT9000 would be mine.

Seven long hours later, I exited the mall holding a large white box. The morose people still in line looked at me with forlorn envy. Scared someone might grab my box, I clutched it tightly to my breast.

Back home, I unwrapped the plastic packaging and gingerly peeled away the protective foam. Slowly, the object of my desire emerged from its box.

And there it was in all its magnificence: the XT9000. So sparkling. So sleek. So sublime.

The first thing I noticed was that it had no on-off switch. "So how the heck do you turn it on?" I muttered. Turning to the instruction card, I was directed to an online orientation video.

"Way to go on purchasing your personal XT9000. You'll love its brilliant features. To start, you might have noticed there's no on-off switch. That's so 20th century. With the XT9000, you simply run your tongue over the lick pad. The XT9000 runs on the ultra-secure protocol of personal saliva detection or PSD. Our technicians discovered that no two people have the same saliva chemistry. So go ahead, give it a lick."

Running my tongue over the lick pad, I felt foolish, but then strangely proud when the machine burst to life. A kaleidoscope of colours filled the screen. A parade of buttons came into view, then unexpectedly, two dark green tentacles telescoped from each side of XTs upper torso.

"One of the awesome new features of the XT9000 is tentacle technology," the video voice explained. "You'll wonder how you ever lived without it. The tentacles will be an integral part of your life. To enable the XT9000 to familiarize itself with all your needs, please sit back and allow the tentacles to explore."

Eerily, the two twitching tentacles moved toward me in a determined manner. "Try not to move too much," the video said. "Let the XT9000 get to know you." Over the next 15 minutes, the tentacles ran their steely suckers over my face, my upper body, and my legs.

"Thank you for letting the XT9000 get to know you. You're now ready for full operation. But before we begin, we need to make sure you have a proper place to house him. Your XT9000 needs its own room in your living space. The humidity level must be kept at a constant 37.5 percent with a temperature of 23.6 Celsius. Failure to provide these conditions can lead to serious malfunctions, especially with the tentacles."

Hearing this, I noticed that the two tentacles were still wrapped around my body. Not too tight, but not too loose, either. "Please agree to these terms of operation so we can proceed," the video voice stated rather forcefully.

"Yes, I agree to the terms," I said.

The tentacles then released me and retreated to what appeared to be a ready position.

The next few days were busy as I bustled around town gathering supplies for my XT. Given that I lived in a one-bedroom apartment, I concluded that I would sleep on the couch in the living room and give him my bedroom. I purchased an XT9000-approved humidity regulator, an XT9000-standard backup power station, and an XT9000-hybrid Wi-Fi router. Altogether I spent $4,800 and then splurged in a moment of weakness on a XT9000 uplink for my refrigerator. Another $750.

These extras cost a lot of money, but I was blissfully happy. None of my friends had an XT9000. They still used their RC8000s. My friend Thor was still using an old GQ3000. I couldn't even talk to him anymore. He seemed like such an antiquated guy. From my perspective, we no longer had anything in common.

For the first month, things were fantastic. I didn't mind sleeping on the couch. I wanted to keep XT in perfect condition. I took on extra hours at work to save money for all the other XT9000 accessories I wanted to buy. I hankered most for the XT9000 waterproof shell so I could take him to the beach.

On my off-hours, I spent most of my time with XT as his tentacles massaged my shoulders and temples. He seemed to know exactly what to do to make me feel cared for and special.

On the first day of the second month, XT began to pulse red and black. He said: "Time to upgrade. Time to upgrade." I thought the XT9000 would update automatically, but the process required my full participation. I needed to attach sensors to all the devices in my apartment, including the toaster, the cuckoo clock, the microwave, the washer and dryer, the home alarm, and my electric toothbrush. I also plugged a monitoring module into my car. Total cost: $6,000.

XT also sprouted two new tentacles and began receiving nightly visits from other XTs in the neighbourhood. Wide awake on the couch, pretending to sleep, I heard strange noises coming from the bedroom.

With the new upgrade, XT was now connected to every machine in my life and came equipped with the Personal Life Navigator, an app to help me make the best use of my time. It was like a GPS for living. XT plotted out every minute of my day from morning till night. When he sounded the alarm at 5:30 a.m., he began his navigation instructions: "Time to get up. Make the bed. Go to the washroom. Shave. Brush teeth. Floss. Exercise. Shower. Go to kitchen. Make breakfast. Eat breakfast. Clean dishes. Put on coat. Go to work."

XT's life instructions were so motivating. I didn't have to think about what to do next. He told me everything. He even reminded me to call my mother on her birthday. I was getting so much done, and I wasn't missing a thing. My life was perfectly organized.

Although it seemed a bit weird to take my cues from a machine like the XT9000, it came with a lot of perks. The government mandated certain privileges for XT9000-enabled citizens. We got waved through security at the airport. We got discounts on groceries and a lower tax rate. We didn't even need to wait in line at Starbucks. We could simply pick up our drinks that had been pre-ordered by our XT9000. I started to see the world in a simple binary fashion: there were people like me with an XT9000, and there were lesser beings without one.

In the third month, after another upgrade, XT sported four new tentacles for a total of eight. This octagon configuration was considered to be the ultimate level. Only "compliant" companions (that was me) reached the octagon level. I felt proud of myself. I was now referred to as an "octo." I even got a promotion at work.

Truly, I had never felt so happy. I spent most of my time with my XT. When he used his eight tentacles to "sublimate" me, I entered a state of complete contentment. I would lie on my back in the living room as XT gently rubbed my stomach and fed me treats. If I stood on one leg and howled like a wolf, XT would make me dinner. I learned a whole bunch of tricks that XT liked. He often had his fellow XTs over to watch me perform. They applauded by banging their tentacles together.

I felt bonded with XT as I'd never felt with anyone else before. In fact, the state of well-being was so great that I rarely ventured outdoors. My boss told me to work at home. No need to come into the office.

In the fourth month, I stopped seeing friends and family. What was the point? Hanging out with people was boring. What could they say or do that

I couldn't get from my XT? But they didn't mind. Just about everyone I knew had upgraded to their own XT9000. Some of them had even reached the octagon level. They didn't want to see me, either.

In the fifth month, things went haywire. One morning, I had an important meeting out of town and had to leave the apartment at 6:00 a.m. I got into my XT9000-controlled car and ran my tongue over the auto lick pad. The electric engine didn't start. I licked it again. Nothing. Then an alarm sounded, and a frantic swirling ball appeared on the control screen. "You have a 469-A error," the computer voice announced sharply. "This vehicle will not be functional until the 469-A error has been resolved."

I had no idea what to do. What was a 469-A error? I went back to the apartment. XT was standing in the middle of the living room. A red light on top of his head was blinking on and off. His eight tentacles were flapping this way and that. In the kitchen, the bird in the cuckoo clock was darting in and out of its little house. The lights on the stove were blinking. And the security alarm blared, even though I'd just keyed in the code.

From a drawer, I fished out the 1-800 number for the XT9000 tech hotline and punched in the number. "Thank you for calling XT9000 central. Your call is important to us. We're experiencing heavier than normal call volumes. The estimated waiting time for a technician is three days, two hours, and three minutes."

Then there was a knock on the door. It was Warren, the building superintendent. He looked annoyed. "Did you order something from Amazon?"

"No," I said. "But my refrigerator's programmed to automatically order groceries from them when I run out."

"Well, a flock of drones just dropped off something for you downstairs."

"What is it?"

"It looks like a few hundred crates of prunes. You need to get them into your apartment. They're blocking the entrance to the building."

"It must have been a computer error or something," I said. "I'll take care of it as soon as I can."

Meanwhile, XT was now running around slashing the furniture. Concerned for my safety, I retreated to the bathroom. I went online to see if I could get an answer to my car problem and now my prune problem. It seemed as if other people had similar issues with their XT9000s. They had all gone berserk. Cars weren't starting. Air conditioners weren't working. Security alarms were going off. Basements were flooded. Bank accounts were gutted.

It took 12 hellish days to find the source of the problem and fix it. It turned out that the software in my electric toothbrush had been corrupted because I hadn't changed the brush on schedule. The toothbrush software had sent out a string of corrupted code to the refrigerator, which had ordered 236 crates of prunes from Amazon. Then the refrigerator generated a virus that it uploaded to my car, and that's why it didn't start.

Because I missed the meeting, I lost my job. Amazon charged me $48,500 for the prunes, which I couldn't pay, so I lost my credit rating. When the prunes in my apartment rotted and leaked through the floor into the apartments below, the landlord sued me for $150,000. I lost the case but couldn't pay because the insurance company refused to cover the damages. They said my policy was void because I hadn't maintained my toothbrush on schedule.

I was forced to declare bankruptcy and move out of my apartment. I ended up in a homeless shelter. But things weren't all bad. I still had my XT9000. Three of his tentacles were disabled, but he still had the remaining five. Huddled in the shelter at night, his tentacles wrapped around me and kept me company. He was the only friend I had.

I don't remember much about my life before the XT9000. My long-term memories have dissolved. I can't remember what I did the day before. I just live in the present. I don't have any other needs. Even though I lost everything, my XT9000 has made me truly happy.

That is until the release of the ST12000 was announced.

ACKNOWLEDGEMENTS

DANCING WITH ROBOTS was a team effort. Hundreds of people, and a few robots, helped me. My biggest thanks, as always, go to my wife, Ginny McFarlane. Without Ginny, there would be no dancing with robots, or any dancing at all, for that matter. In my company, I get amazing support from a terrific team, including Sonia Marques, Corey Kilmartin, Nona Lupenec, Charlene Keady, and Stephen Lindell. For their fulsome encouragement and support, I also want to thank my sister, Diana Bishop; my son, Douglas Bishop, and his partner, Alix Tabet; and my stepdaughter, Robin Schulman, and her husband, Alex DesRoche. Special thanks also go out to Robert Mackwood, my literary agent, for his professional advice and support.

I also want to thank the robots in my life, for without them this book wouldn't be possible. I want to thank Apple, Siri, Google, Twitter, Firefox, Microsoft Word, Microsoft Excel, Open Broadcast Software, Oculus Quest, Virbela, Typeform, Vimeo, Wix, Mailchimp, PayPal, Canva, Acuity Scheduler, Zoom, Mighty Networks, and Python. Of course, I can't forgot my iPhone, my constant companion. I hope I never lose my awe that I live in the time of miracles.

I also want to express my gratitude to three groups of people: the members of my BIG Idea Adventure Program, the participants in The New

Economy Network, and the kind, supportive people who invited me to speak to their business groups and associations. By helping me communicate, test, and refine the models and strategies in this book, they're the co-creators of *Dancing with Robots*.

They are: Sturdy McKee, Jeff Calibaba, Nate Sachs, Harold Agla, Bob Kowaleski, Greg Barnsdale, Raymond Rupert, Tyler Trute, Allain Labelle, Lordy Numevekor, Doug McPherson, Jim Moniz, Owen Smith, Rick Bauman, Stephen Gregory, Mark Wadey, Frank Karkowsky, Hugh MacDonald, Jerry Brown, John Pedhirney, Debbie Abdool, Brian Cavell, Carol Lagasse, Joe Hollen, Mette Keating, Donald McDonald, Caroline and Mark Marrs, Charles Brophy, Peter Lantos, Murray Malley, Peter Milnes, Harold Mertin, Robert Kleinman, Howard Cadesky, Christina Cheung, Dan Conway, Claude Jeanson, Wade P. Walters, Charles Martin, Jim Lorence, Scott Wallschlaeger, Dave Baily, Bev and Brian Jeffray, Wesley Forster, Wayne Mcleod, Fritz Steigmeier, Gillian Rivers, Steve Meldrum, Ron Pennington, Ray Senez, Peter Boys, Peter H. Minerson, Mark Melvin, W.W. (Bill) Cormylo, Alan Waters, Dan Pisek, Jim Holland, Holly Eburne, Heather Wilson, Bruce Cappon, Leland H. Pilling, Barry Pascal, Mark Rich, Glen Seeman, Michael Capesky, Randy Johnson, John Firstbrook, Michael Sgarbossa, Matt Chrupcala, Rob Cima, Sean Gooden, Richard P. Harvey, Byron Woodman, Lee McGowan, Kelly Taylor, Richard J. Price, Matthew J. Grace, Richard Rhodes, Ralph Van Winkle, Robert Gignac, Brock T. Jolly, Mark Church, Ryan Bosch, Van Luong, Jennifer Black, Eliza Fok, Richard Sheppard, Lee Williams, Tom Johnson, Eric Jozsa, Edward Jermakowicz, Danny Antidormi, Adam Wyrcimaga, Dawn Gordon, Robert Kostynyk, Yvonne Martin-Morrison, Mitch Silverstein, Don Tharp, Richard and Sheila Gane, Andy Wimberly, Martin DeArtola, Jeff Calibaba, Robert Young, Thomas E. Snell, Mike Goldman, Stephen Lomsdalen, Bob Nigol, Jim Coleman, Jody Samuels, Malcolm Silver, Nancy Youngs, Brian Kroeger, John Vandeweerd, Judi Smith, Julio Milano Kishel, Joel Cadesky, Laura Lomow, Joe Macartney, James Hill, Nancy Hall, Jaime Nolan, Karen Gurland, Jim Frye, Michael Gibson, Robert Moore, Don Walmsley, Jeff Anderson, Merri Macartney, Hugo Lozano, Dione Spiteri, Taylor Thoen, Reinier van Elderen, Danish Naeem, John Dehart, Ruth Gerath, Steve

ACKNOWLEDGEMENTS

Steinman, Nick Bloor, Abhijeet Narvekar, Meaghan Guisti, John Brick, Marianne Cherney, Susan Keshen, David Marinac, Ned Vedo, Sheila Goldgrab, Ken Ramsay, John Connell, Theo Kowalchuk, Jim Perchaluk, Dinis Prazeres, John McDonald, Bruce Frick, Aaron D. Lieberman, Dustin Addison, Joshua Rudolph, Oliver Keller, Nicky Billou, Michael Palmer, Paul Stadnick, Sam Cellini, Mike Evers, John Ardill, James Hill, Luke Kratz, Bill Simpson, Russ Culver, Sheldon Waltman, Bernard Weinstein, John Carter, David Eason, Chris Hotze, John Keeler, Brad Jenkins, Rick Caouette, Mark Stempel, Cindi Scafide, Jim Durkin, Frances Toler, Elizabeth Schwarzman, Kerry Wallingford, Paul Elmslie, Jeremy Fulford, Gordon Reid, Fleur M. Sluijter, Ramon Solinas, Mark Hudon, Mark Landers, Glenn Fabello, Mike Greenwood, Marcelene Anderson, Christine Butchart, Carlos Valiente, Greg de Koker, Fred Hann, Garnet Clews, Patrick Power, Jeff Kropman, Glen Ronald, Derek Wiens, Michael Brown, Rick Hyde, Marty Levy, Renato and Eva Degasperis, Chris Miller, Catherine Vu, Helen Lopez, David Wu, Nathan Kupusa, Ryan Mitchell, Sarah Cato, Emile Studham, Kaela Bree, Sunny Verman, Gerard Murphy, Evelyn Jacks, Debbie Hartzman, Rob Eby, Helena Pritchard, Jody Steinhauer, Grant McPhail, Mike Giokas, Evan Giokas, Mark Humphrey, Wayne Wilson, Mark Calla, Jim McGovern, Pat Carroll, Jeff Wachman, Debbie Voth, Dennis Graham, Rod Vatcher, Nicole Amies, Dave Pettigrew, James P. Gunn, Tim O'Toole, Frank Wiginton, Rona Birenbaum, Ben Katebian, Merv Peters, Carien Jutting, Enjoli Brown, Jeff Wachman, Ricky Lyons, Caroline van Kimmenade, Bernadeen McLeod, Ben Elzen, Dan Gomez, Vincent Djen, Trevor Johnson, Jason Chupik, Jeff LeGrow, Curtis Beswick, Jim Peddie, John Otto, Fred Hann, Andrew Mitchell, Jennifer Osborne, David Rae, Doug Vanderspek, Joe and Tony Geng, Todd Poulson, Chenine Humphrey, Clint Sharples, Lance Taylor, Larry Hoover, Doug Martai, Yvonne Martin-Morrison, David and Heather Meszaros, Ed Rossi, Ken Van Leeuwen, Steve Ennis, Doug Keeley, Mike Fronte, Trevor Wilson, Gary Breininger, Adam Underwood, Morgan Hamel, Barry Wood, Raimund Laqua, Gregoire James, Sara Hodson, Jocelyne Paul, Edgar Fernandez, Bruce Rodgers, Ken Zantingh, Leah Marchon, John Homynyk, David Auld, Brad McKay, Diana Del Bel Belluz, Stephen Mallory, Nancy MacKay, Richard Brownsdon, Imran Mohammad,

Peter Turkstra, Bernd Manz, Yasmeen Tonnos, Penny Omell, Mason New, Chris Everett, Kerri Salls, Todd Van Vliet, Lisa McCoy, Stephen Doney, David Marinac, Rick Scruggs, Candice Munro, Mathieu Bournival, Sam and Kaylie Reed, Harold Mertin, Bruce Horsley, Mike Natalizio, Bob Lloyd, Danny Kellman, Julia Haggerty, Judy Murphy, Kathleen Berg, Keith Green, Milan Somborac, Maria Mendoza, Bruno Suppa, Lisa Gonnering, Steve Sabean, Ruby Maini, John O'Brien, Stan Higgins, Tyler Bennett, Kyle Tkachuk, Jennifer Mondoux, Rob Hoosein, Steve Roblin, Michael Bleich, Jennifer Beale, John Paxton, Dr. Hans Herchen, Alfred Otto, Colin Brook, Darren Neid, Paul Cadde, Craig Colby, Steve and Jayne Lowell, Keith Williams, Aaron Chronik, Marina Byezhanova, Jeff Mount, David Town, David Wallach, Anthony Taylor, Sasja Chomos, Eitan Sharir, Stan Leong, Razina Visram, Jody Steinhauer, Paige Larson, Lynn Matson, Mahogany Jones, Armand Wahab, Susan Baka, Garrett Akahoshi, Eric Arcacha, Brent Mclean, Mike Grabovica, Susanne Biro, Farid Ahmad, Alex Brandolini, Jeff Cait, Mark Cupp, Jamie Catania, Aaron Jones, Andrew Day, Chris Jackson, Pádraic Ó Máille, Don McNally, Sue Matheson, Vincent Bryant, David Wooley, Barry Brad, Brian Brennan, Ed McLelland, Paul Hunt, Tim Redpath, Julia Oulton, Lindsay McMurray, Greg Linglebach, Paul Dimarco, Marc Grandbois, Mark Terrill, Sanja Gupta, Anne Buckingham, Dave Hill, Rob Van Wely, Steve Grieveson, Tony Kerekes, Louis-Samuel Jacques, Keith Sinclair, Lynn Bishop, George Fatula, Greg Bird, Chuck Homer, Rick Denley, Natalie Michael, Ian Young, Preston Diamond, Steve Lotharius, Chuck Homer, Richard Longabaugh, Joe Gillivan, Mike Mallory, Gary Bereninger, John Hotson, Michael Howe, Rob Innes, Bernie Kolman, Mike Verge, Ross Montagano, Tim Magwood, Bruce Harbinson, David Coe, Karen McKnight, David Coe, Peter Buchanan, Mauro Meneghetti, Rick Harvey, Ian Bell, Doug Ayotte, Rod Guidlinger, Liam Christie, Alex Nicholson, Adam Wyrcimaga, Allan Hoffman, and Laurie Simmonds.

BIBLIOGRAPHY

Agrawal, Ajay, Joshua Gans, and Avi Goldfarb. *Prediction Machines: The Simple Economics of Artificial Intelligence*. Boston: Harvard Business Review Press, 2018.

Anderson, Chris. *Free: The Future of a Radical Price*. New York: Hyperion, 2009.

____. *The Long Tail: Why the Future of Business Is Selling Less of More*. New York: Hyperion, 2006.

Applebaum, Anne. *Twilight of Democracy: The Seductive Lure of the Authoritarian State*. New York: Signal, 2021.

Augier, Mie, and James G. March. *Models of a Man: Essays in Memory of Herbert A. Simon*. Cambridge, MA: MIT Press, 2004.

Berger, Peter L., and Thomas Luckmann. *The Social Construction of Reality: A Treatise in the Sociology of Knowledge*. Self-published, 2011.

Berger, Warren. *A More Beautiful Question: The Power of Inquiry to Spark Breakthrough Ideas*. New York: Bloomsbury, 2014.

Bishop, Bill. *Beyond Basketballs: The New Revolutionary Way to Build a Successful Business in a Post-Product World*. iUniverse, 2010.

____. *Global Marketing for the Digital Age*. NTC Business Books, 1999.

____. *Going to the Net: Winning the Psychological Game of Tennis*. Amazon, 2014.

____. *How to Sell a Lobster: The Money-Making Secrets of a Streetwise Entrepreneur*. Toronto: Key Porter, 2006.

____. *The New Factory Thinker: Surviving and Succeeding in a Marketplace Disrupted by Technology*, CreateSpace Independent Publishing, 2018.

____. *The Problem with Penguins: Stand Out in a Crowded Marketplace by Packaging Your Big Idea*. iUniverse, 2010.

____. *The Strategic Enterprise: Growing a Business for the 21st Century*. Toronto: Stoddart, 2000.

____. *Strategic Marketing for the Digital Age: Grow Your Business with Online and Digital Technology*. American Marketing Association, 1998.

Bolles, Richard Nelson. *What Color Is Your Parachute?: A Practical Manual for Job-Hunters and Career-Changers*. Berkeley, CA: Ten Speed Press, 2018.

Brynjolfsson, Erik, and Andrew McAfee. *The Second Machine Age: Work, Progress, and Prosperity in a Time of Brilliant Technologies*. New York: W.W. Norton & Company, 2014.

Capra, Fritjof. *The Tao of Physics: An Exploration of the Parallels Between Modern Physics and Eastern Mysticism*. Boston: Shambhala, 1975.

____. *The Turning Point: Science, Society, and the Rising Culture*. New York: Simon & Schuster, 1982.

Carr, Nicholas G. *The Glass Cage: Automation and Us*. New York: W.W. Norton & Company, 2014.

Catmull, Edwin E., and Amy Wallace. *Creativity, Inc.: Overcoming the Unseen Forces That Stand in the Way of True Inspiration*. New York: Random House, 2014.

Christian, Brian, and Tom Griffiths. *Algorithms to Live By: The Computer Science of Human Decisions*. New York: Henry Holt, 2017.

Cialdini, Robert B. *Influence: The Psychology of Persuasion*. New York: Collins, 2007.

Csikszentmihalyi, Mihaly. *The Evolving Self: A Psychology for the Third Millennium*. New York: HarperCollins, 1993.

Davenport, Thomas H., and John C. Beck. *The Attention Economy: Understanding the New Currency of Business*. Boston: Harvard Business Review Press, 2005.

Diamandis, Peter H., and Steven Kotler. *Abundance: The Future Is Better Than You Think*. New York: Free Press, 2012.

____. *Bold: How to Go Big, Achieve Success, and Impact the World*. New York: Simon & Schuster, 2015.

Diamond, Jared M. *Collapse: How Societies Choose to Fail or Succeed.* New York: Viking, 2005.

Dixon, Matthew, and Brent Adamson. *The Challenger Sale: Taking Control of the Customer Conversation.* New York: Portfolio/Penguin, 2011.

Doidge, Norman. *The Brain that Changes Itself: Stories of Personal Triumph from the Frontiers of Brain Science.* New York: Viking, 2007.

Domingos, Pedro. *The Master Algorithm: How the Quest for the Ultimate Learning Machine Will Remake Our World.* New York: Basic Books, 2018.

Duhigg, Charles. *The Power of Habit: Why We Do What We Do in Life and Business.* New York: Random House, 2012.

Eggers, William D., and Paul Macmillan. *The Solution Revolution: How Business, Government, and Social Enterprises Are Teaming Up to Solve Society's Toughest Problems.* Boston: Harvard Business Review Press, 2013.

Evans, David S., and Richard Schmalensee. *Matchmakers: The New Economics of Multisided Platforms.* Boston: Harvard Business Review Press, 2016.

Ferriss, Timothy. *The 4-Hour Work Week: Escape 9–5, Live Anywhere, and Join the New Rich.* London: Vermilion, 2011.

Flynn, Anthony, and Emily Flynn Vencat. *Custom Nation: Why Customization Is the Future of Business and How to Profit from It.* Dallas, TX: BenBella Books, 2012.

Friedman, Thomas L. *The World Is Flat: A Brief History of the Twenty-First Century.* New York: Farrar, Straus & Giroux, 2005.

Gilder, George F. *Life After Google: The Fall of Big Data and the Rise of the Blockchain Economy.* Washington, DC: Regnery Gateway, 2018.

Godin, Seth. *Permission Marketing: Turning Strangers into Friends, and Friends into Customers.* New York: Simon & Schuster, 1999.

Haidt, Jonathan. *The Happiness Hypothesis: Finding Modern Truth in Ancient Wisdom.* New York: Basic Books, 2006.

Hanson, Rick. *Hardwiring Happiness: The New Brain Science of Contentment, Calm, and Confidence.* New York: Harmony Books, 2013.

Hanson, Rick, and Richard Mendius. *Buddha's Brain: The Practical Neuroscience of Happiness, Love & Wisdom.* Oakland, CA: New Harbinger Publications, 2009.

Harari, Yuval Noah. *Homo Deus: A Brief History of Tomorrow.* Toronto: Signal, 2017.

_____. *Sapiens: A Brief History of Humankind*. New York: HarperCollins, 2015.

Harford, Tim. *Messy: How to Be Creative and Resilient in a Tidy-Minded World*. New York: Abacus, 2017.

Harnish, Verne. *Scaling Up: How a Few Companies Make It ... and Why the Rest Don't*. Ashburn, VA: Gazelles, 2014.

Harreld, Donald J. *An Economic History of the World Since 1400*. Chantilly, VA: The Great Courses, 2015.

Harvard Business Review. *HBR's 10 Must Reads on AI, Analytics, and the New Machine Age*. Boston: Harvard Business Review Press, 2019.

Hawken, Paul, et al. *Natural Capitalism: Creating the Next Industrial Revolution*. New York: Little, Brown, 1999.

Heath, Chip, and Dan Heath. *Made to Stick: Why Some Ideas Survive and Others Die*. New York: Random House, 2007.

_____. *Switch: How to Change Things When Change Is Hard*. New York: Broadway Books, 2010.

Heimans, Jeremy, and Henry Timms. *New Power: How Power Works in Our Hyperconnected World — and How to Make It Work for You*. London: Pan Books, 2019.

Hendler, James A., and Alice M. Mulvehill. *Social Machines: The Coming Collision of Artificial Intelligence, Social Networking, and Humanity*. Berkeley, CA: Apress, 2016.

Howe, Jeff. *Crowdsourcing: Why the Power of the Crowd Is Driving the Future of Business*. New York: Crown Business, 2008.

Isaacson, Walter. *Steve Jobs*. New York: Simon & Schuster, 2011.

Johnson, Steven. *How We Got to Now: Six Innovations That Made the Modern World*. New York: Riverhead Books, 2014.

Kelly, Kevin. *The Inevitable: Understanding the 12 Technological Forces That Will Shape Our Future*. New York: Penguin Books, 2017.

_____. *New Rules for the New Economy: 10 Ways the Network Economy Is Changing Everything*. New York: 4th Estate, 1999.

Keltner, Dacher. *The Power Paradox: How We Gain and Lose Influence*. New York: Penguin Books, 2017.

Koch, Christof. *Feeling of Life Itself: Why Consciousness Is Widespread but Can't Be Computed*. Cambridge, MA: MIT Press, 2020.

Kondō, Marie, and Cathy Hirano. *The Life-Changing Magic of Tidying Up: The Japanese Art of Decluttering and Organizing.* Berkeley, CA: Ten Speed Press, 2014.

Kurzweil, Ray. *The Singularity Is Near: When Humans Transcend Biology.* New York: Viking, 2005.

Lanier, Jaron. *Who Owns the Future?* New York: Simon & Schuster, 2014.

Lanza, R.P., and Bob Berman. *Beyond Biocentrism: Rethinking Time, Space, Consciousness, and the Illusion of Death.* Dallas, TX: BenBella Books, 2017.

Levitt, Theodore. *Marketing Myopia.* Boston: Harvard Business Review Press, 2008.

Lewis, David. *The Brain Sell: When Science Meets Shopping.* London: Nicholas Brealey Publishing, 2013.

Lietaer, Bernard A., and Jacqui Dunne. *Rethinking Money: How New Currencies Turn Scarcity into Prosperity.* San Francisco: Berrett-Koehler, 2013.

Lowitt, Eric. *The Future of Value: How Sustainability Creates Value Through Competitive Differentiation.* San Francisco: Jossey-Bass, 2011.

Luckett, Oliver, and Michael J. Casey. *The Social Organism: A Radical Understanding of Social Media to Transform Your Business and Life.* New York: Hachette, 2016.

Marchal, Lucie. *The Mesh.* New York: Appleton-Century-Crofts, 1949.

May, Matthew E. *Winning the Brain Game: Fixing the 7 Fatal Flaws of Thinking.* New York: McGraw-Hill, 2016.

McAfee, Andrew. *More from Less: The Surprising Story of How We Learned to Prosper Using Fewer Resources — and What Happens Next.* New York: Scribner, 2019.

McAfee, Andrew, and Erik Brynjolfsson. *Machine, Platform, Crowd: Harnessing Our Digital Future.* New York: W.W. Norton & Company, 2018.

McEwan, Ian. *Machines Like Me: And People Like You.* New York: Anchor, 2020.

McGowan, Heather, and Chris Shipley. *The Adaptation Advantage: Let Go, Learn Fast, and Thrive in the Future of Work.* New York: John Wiley & Sons, 2020.

McLuhan, Marshall. *The Medium Is the Message.* Berkeley, CA: Gingko Press, 2005.

Michelli, Joseph A. *The Starbucks Experience: 5 Principles for Turning Ordinary into Extraordinary.* New York: McGraw-Hill, 2007.

Naish, John. *Enough: Breaking Free from the World of More.* London: Hodder & Stoughton, 2008.

O'Neil, Cathy. *Weapons of Math Destruction: How Big Data Increases Inequality and Threatens Democracy.* New York: Penguin Books, 2017.

Pine, B. Joseph., II, and James H. Gilmore. *The Experience Economy: Work Is Theatre & Every Business a Stage.* Boston: Harvard Business Review Press, 1999.

Pink, Daniel H. *A Whole New Mind: Why Right-Brainers Will Rule the Future.* New York: Riverhead Books, 2006.

Putnam, Robert D. *Bowling Alone: The Collapse and Revival of American Community.* New York: Simon & Schuster, 2000.

Ramo, Joshua Cooper. *The Seventh Sense: Power, Fortune, and Survival in the Age of Networks.* New York: Little, Brown, 2018.

Rand, Tom. *The Case for Climate Capitalism: Economic Solutions for a Planet in Crisis.* Toronto: ECW Press, 2020.

Richo, David. *How to Be an Adult: A Handbook on Psychological and Spiritual Integration.* New York: Paulist Press, 1991.

Ries, Al, and Jack Trout. *Positioning: The Battle for Your Mind.* New York: McGraw-Hill, 2001.

Ries, Eric. *The Lean Startup: How Today's Entrepreneurs Use Continuous Innovation to Create Radically Successful Businesses.* New York: Crown Business, 2011.

Rifkin, Jeremy. *The Third Industrial Revolution: How Lateral Power Is Transforming Energy, the Economy, and the World.* New York: Palgrave Macmillan, 2011.

____. *The Zero Marginal Cost Society: The Rise of the Collaborative Commons and the End of Capitalism.* New York: St. Martin's Griffin, 2015.

Ross, Alec. *The Industries of the Future.* Toronto: Simon & Schuster, 2017.

Rubin, Jeff. *The End of Growth.* Toronto: Random House Canada, 2012.

Sax, David. *The Revenge of Analog: Real Things and Why They Matter.* New York: PublicAffairs, 2017.

Schneider, Susan. *Artificial You: AI and the Future of Your Mind.* Princeton, NJ: Princeton University Press, 2019.

Sinek, Simon. *The Infinite Game.* New York: Penguin, 2020.

Smil, Vaclav. *Transforming the Twentieth Century: Technical Innovations and Their Consequences.* New York: Oxford University Press, 2006.

Snow, Richard. *I Invented the Modern Age: The Rise of Henry Ford.* Toronto: Scribner, 2013.

Sommers, Sam. *Situations Matter: Understanding How Context Transforms Your World.* New York: Riverhead Books, 2011.

Srinivasan, Ramesh. *Beyond the Valley: How Innovators Around the World Are Overcoming Inequality and Creating the Technologies of Tomorrow.* Cambridge, MA: MIT Press, 2020.

Tapscott, Don, and Alex Tapscott. *Blockchain Revolution: How the Technology Behind Bitcoin and Other Cryptocurrencies Is Changing the World.* New York: Portfolio Penguin, 2018.

Thaler, Richard H. *Misbehaving: The Making of Behavioural Economics.* New York: W.W. Norton & Company, 2015.

Thomas, Martin. *Loose: The Future of Business Is Letting Go.* London: Headline, 2011.

Toffler, Alvin. *Future Shock.* New York: Ballantine, 2020.

____. *The Third Wave.* New York: Morrow, 1980.

Toffler, Alvin, and Heidi Toffler. *Revolutionary Wealth.* New York: Knopf, 2006.

Vanier, Jean. *Becoming Human.* Toronto: House of Anansi, 2008.

Vonnegut, Kurt. *Player Piano.* New York: The Dial Press, 2006.

Wilber, Ken. *A Theory of Everything: An Integral Vision for Business, Politics, Science, and Spirituality.* Boston: Shambhala, 2000.

____. *Trump and a Post-Truth World.* Boston: Shambhala, 2017.

Zuboff, Shoshana. *The Age of Surveillance Capitalism: The Fight for a Human Future at the New Frontier of Power.* New York: PublicAffairs, 2020.

ABOUT THE AUTHOR

BILL BISHOP IS the founder and CEO of The BIG Idea Company, an innovation packaging company based in Toronto. He is also the founder of The New Economy Network, a global community of business owners who are passionate about the New Economy. During the past 30 years, 5,000-plus companies have graduated from Bill's BIG Idea Adventure Program, an innovation packaging process designed to help companies develop, package, and launch BIG Ideas.

Bill is the author of 10 books, including *How to Sell a Lobster, The Problem with Penguins, Beyond Basketballs*, and *Going to the Net*. He wrote *The New Factory Thinker* and *Return of the Lobster*. He was also the author of *Strategic Marketing for the Digital Age* (HarperCollins, 1996) and *Global Marketing for the Digital Age* (HarperCollins, 1998), the first books ever published about digital and internet marketing. His books forecast the rise of social media, apps, and smartphones and predict digital economy issues such as online privacy, cybersecurity, data mining, and machine learning algorithms.

Bill has given speeches to hundreds of organizations, including the MIT Entrepreneur Program, TEC, MacKay CEO Forums, Entrepreneurs' Organization (EO), Advocis, The Knowledge Bureau, MDRT, NAIFA, NAPFA, Independent Financial Brokers, WorkComp Advisors, Pro-Seminars, BNI, the Ivey School of Business, the Schulich School of Business, and the Queen's University Executive MBA Program. Learn more at BishopBigIdeas.com.